# GEORGIA BONESTEEL'S
# *Bright Ideas*
## *for*
# LAP QUILTING

Oxmoor House

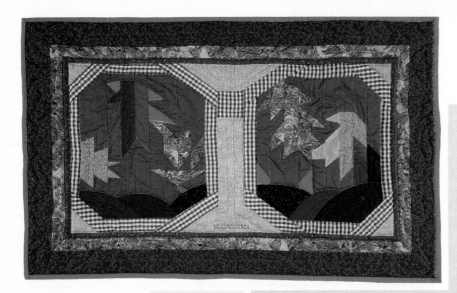

To quiltmakers
and quilt dreamers:
Let your vision
seek out bright
ideas.

Library of Congress Catalog Number: 90-61776
ISBN: 0-8487-1003-7
Manufactured in the United States of America
First Printing 1990

Executive Editor: Nancy J. Fitzpatrick
Director of Manufacturing: Jerry Higdon
Associate Production Manager: Rick Litton
Art Director: Bob Nance
Copy Chief: Mary Jean Haddin

*Bright Ideas for Lap Quilting*

Editor: Susan Ramey Wright
Contributing Editor: Charlotte Hagood
Assistant Editor: Virginia A. Welch
Senior Designer: Earl Freedle
Photo Stylist: Katie Stoddard
Assistant Copy Editor: Susan Smith Cheatham
Editorial Assistant: Alice L. Cox
Production Assistant: Theresa L. Beste
Senior Photographer: John O'Hagan
Additional Photography: Gary Clark, Vann Cleveland,
Colleen Duffley, Mary-Gray Hunter, Bruce Roberts
Artists: Samuel L. Baldwin, Larry Hunter

# CONTENTS

# INSPIRATION

When our foremothers sat down with their hoarded fabric scraps and worn clothing to make warm covers, they had no books or store-bought patterns to help them create their quilts. Instead, they looked to their imaginations. Their patterns reflected the things they saw around them every day: flying geese, turkeys, bears, mountain peaks, ocean waves, starry skies, log walls. Some patterns also came from the pages of the Bible—the only book many families owned. Jacob's Ladder, Crown of Thorns, and Star of Bethlehem are a few.

*Bright Ideas for Lap Quilting* is meant to stir your creative juices and help you find the inspiration to design your own patchwork. Explore the world around you to find ideas for original quilts, but hold fast to the time-honored quilting traditions that the mothers of our craft invented out of necessity.

The life of today's quilter is often a balancing act between her craft and her everyday activities. But those activities can be much more than a source of irritation. The talented quilter can find bright ideas in even the most mundane corners of her life.

*"Sew along with me; the best quilts are yet to be."*

*One of my favorite folk art sculptures is this piece called* The Balancing Act. *It reminds me of the balancing act that today's quilter must perform between her craft and the other interests and responsibilities that claim her time and mental energies.*

## Sources Far and Near

Ideas for quilts can come from your imagination or memory, deriving from dreams or past events. Or they can be born of any of thousands of sensory experiences. Stimuli are everywhere—in music, art, nature, advertising, children at play, household pets—anywhere there is something to see or hear or feel.

*Some of the best quilt design inspirations could be right under your feet. I incorporated this floor tile pattern into the* Masks, Moose, and Qupak *quilt on page 46.*

To record new visual images, take your camera along on vacations and use it liberally. Landscapes and seascapes offer many design possibilities. Explore shops, museums, architecture, and local customs for ideas. These sights can influence style, design, and color, allowing you to grow in your craft.

My teaching experiences on cruise ships gave me the ideas for three of the quilts in this book:

*Cruise and Quilt Banner*, page 52; *The Big Ship*, page 54; and *Moonbeams Over Many Ports*, page 56. A visit to Alaska gave birth to *Masks, Moose, and Qupak.*

Just like our foremothers, we can find bright ideas for quilts in our own backyards. Houses, shops, sidewalks, flower gardens, autumn leaves—all the everyday sights and sounds in our hometowns can provide material for quilt designs.

*Just look out your window. Nature's bounty will inspire you. In reading about the* Autumn Windows *quilt on page 22, you'll learn how a box of colorful autumn leaves, sent across the miles from a friend, provided the bright idea for a magnificent quilt.*

*What better place to relax and have fun than on a cruise ship! But even when relaxing, keep your quilt brain awake for quilt design possibilities. As you'll see in the "Vacation Quilts" chapter of this book, some of my favorite quilt designs were inspired at sea.*

## The Geometrics

Beginners often ask me for the easiest patterns. Students entering contests want some tips for winning designs. I always tell them to, "Study the geometrics."

You'll find geometric patterns all around you. Mountains, trees, houses, boats, even animals—all are made up of circles, squares, triangles, and rectangles.

*Beautiful landscapes like this Smoky Mountain scene can spark new quilt designs. Mountains, valleys, and celestial bodies are full of geometric patterns. And even a child can find enchantment in clouds.*

## Shop for Bright Ideas

Never pass up a drafting supply shop or the art and design section of a college bookstore. These stores routinely stock a potpourri of books and supplies with strong design orientation. Designs from such books grew into the bands of colored cloth that dominate the string quilts in the "String Fever" chapter.

Study the designs of other crafts such as stained glass making, needlepoint, and rug hooking to get crossover ideas for your favorite craft. And the ultimate inspiration may be a leisurely visit to the fabric store. Stroll through the aisles of fabric bolts, getting lost in the colors, textures, and designs.

## The Truest Form of Originality

Sometimes new quilts emerge from past mistakes. I misplaced a triangle in my first attempt at the *Star Glaze* quilt. So I felt compelled to remake it. This time around I changed the border design and introduced a larger print to make the quilt on page 34.

Perhaps imitation is the sincerest form of flattery, but making a mistake is one of the truest forms of originality.

## Stay Open to New Ideas

Don't be afraid to experiment. Gambling with a unique fabric or turning a block sideways can be the "Voila!" or "Eureka!" experience that makes your quilt special.

*Quilt blocks need not be cast in stone—as these are. The beautiful Ferguson Fountain at Mars Hill College, Mars Hill, North Carolina, stands eight feet tall and more than 20 feet wide. Its 280 ceramic tiles depict 84 traditional quilt block designs from quilts made by Appalachian Mountain women.*

Attitude is a critical part of quiltmaking. Never say never. What you imagined could never happen, just might! To me, compass designs always seemed impossible to re-create in cloth. But with dogged perseverance, I did it! Not once, but twice, in *Golden Threads, Silver Needles I* and *II*.

Keep an open mind for anything and everything new in the way of fabrics, patterns, and techniques. Remember that stretching your mind and attitude is the first step in creating special quilts.

Our quilt well will never run dry as long as we search, think, dream, and desire. There are as many new quilts to be made as there are sets of hands to make them.

Come on, sew along with me; the best quilts are yet to be.

*Let your imagination be your mental lighthouse, lighting the way to quilting masterpieces.*

*When broken down into its simplest parts, basic geometric shapes, a compass design like the ones in the "Warm the Walls" chapter becomes a puzzle in patchwork that is solved as seams join.*

# HOMETOWN QUILTS

You can wander far and wide, but isn't it a surprise when you find inspiration right outside your own back door?

*Bricktown*

# Bricktown

While I was in Alaska, class member Pam Bickford adapted the herringbone brick pattern to a piecing design. I have used that design in *Bricktown*.

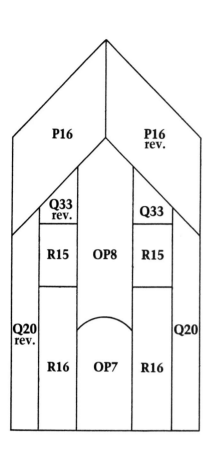

Finished Size: 38" x 72"
Perimeter: 220"
Blocks: 7 (8½" x 17") House blocks
  •   2 (4¼" x 17") Half-house
        blocks

**Fabric Requirements:**

| | |
|---|---|
| Large black print | ¾ yard |
| White print | 2¼ yards |
| Pink moiré | ¾ yard |
| Dk. blue print | ¾ yard |
| Small black print | ¾ yard |
| Teal | ⅜ yard |
| Black check | ⅜ yard |
| Backing | 2¼ yards |
| Teal for binding | ¾ yard |

**Pieces to Cut:**

| | |
|---|---|
| OP7 | 9 white print |
| OP8 | 2 large black print |
| | 2 pink moiré |
| | 2 dk. blue print |
| | 2 small black print |

| | |
|---|---|
| P16 | 8 teal |
| | 8 black check* |
| Q20 | 4 large black print** |
| | 4 pink moiré** |
| | 4 dk. blue print** |
| | 4 small black print** |
| Q24 | 3 large black print |
| | 3 white print |
| | 3 pink moiré |
| | 3 dk. blue print |
| | 3 small black print |
| Q33 | 4 large black print** |
| | 4 pink moiré** |
| | 4 dk. blue print** |
| | 4 small black print** |
| R7 | 21 large black print |
| | 21 white print |

| | |
|---|---|
| | 21 pink moiré |
| | 21 dk. blue print |
| | 21 small black print |
| R15 | 16 white print |
| R16 | 4 large black print |
| | 4 pink moiré |
| | 4 dk. blue print |
| | 4 small black print |
| T46 | 3 large black print |
| | 3 white print |
| | 3 pink moiré |
| | 3 dk. blue print |
| | 3 small black print |
| 2½" x 72½" strip | |
| | 2 white print |

*Reverse template.
**Reverse template for half the pieces.

## Quilt Construction:

**1.** Following block diagram on page 11 for placement, make 7 house blocks and 2 half-house blocks. When joining P16 unit (roof) to roof line of house, stitch from side of house to corner dot at roof peak. Backstitch. Break off thread. Insert needle at corner dot on opposite side of seam allowance and stitch to other side of house. To make half-house blocks, mark vertical center lines on OP7 and OP8 templates. Add seam allowance to center edge of each half-template.

**2.** To make center section, start piecing at bottom edge of Row 1 (see Diagram 1). Join strip 1 (large black print Q24) to strip 2 (white print R7). Leave final ½" of seam unstitched as shown in Diagram 2, Figure 1.

Join strip 3 (pink moiré Q24) as shown in Diagram 2, Figure 2, stitching entire length of seam. Join strip 4 (dk. blue R7), leaving final ½" of seam unstitched as shown in Diagram 2, Figure 3. Continue adding strips in same manner, following the 5-color sequence in photograph.

**3.** Referring to Diagram 1, piece 4 panels as shown, using Q24 and R7 pieces on Row 1, R7 pieces on Rows 2 and 3, and R7 and T46 pieces on Row 4. (Join T46 triangles to R7 rectangles before completing Row 4.) Leave final ½" of seams unstitched on *both* sides of Rows 2 and 3.

**4.** Join Rows 1 and 2, beginning at top of panels and working down. (Match edge by using notches in Diagram 1.) Join Row 2 to Row 3 and Row 3 to Row 4 to complete center section.

**5.** Join house blocks as shown in photograph. Join house rows to top and bottom edges of center section.

**6.** Join side borders to quilt.

**7.** Machine-quilt with a feather stitch as shown in photograph. Hand-quilt a scallop design in roof area. Bind with teal fabric.

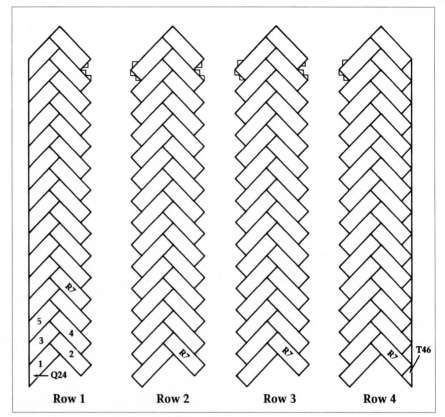

**Diagram 1: Assembling and Joining Rows**

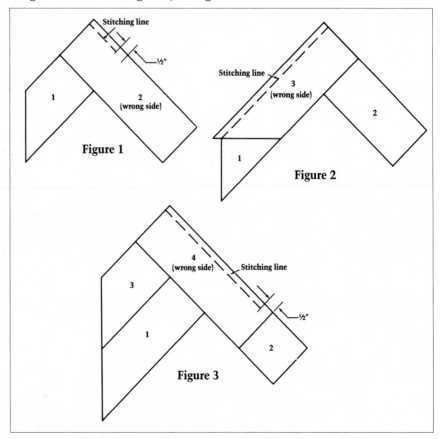

**Diagram 2: Piecing Rows**

# Dewey Decimal 746

The library is a wonderful source of quilting information! Here's a trivia tidbit that all quilters should know. The Dewey decimal number for all quilting books is 746. Check it out—anywhere, in any hometown.

This friendship quilt was made by the Landrum Library Quilters in Landrum, South Carolina, for their retiring librarian, Ruth Farrar. Each book is made from a different calico, and each quilter's name is stitched into her book's spine.

Finished Size: 74" x 84"
Perimeter: 316"
Blocks: 42 (10"-square) Book blocks

**Fabric Requirements:**

| | |
|---|---|
| Assorted prints and solids | 1¾ yards total |
| Muslin | 3¾ yards |
| Dk. blue print | 1½ yards |
| Rose print | 2½ yards |
| Backing | 5 yards |
| Dk. blue print for binding | ⅞ yard |

**Pieces to Cut:**

| | |
|---|---|
| OP12 | 42 muslin |
| OP17 | 42 dk. blue print |
| P15 | 84 assorted prints* |
| R4 | 42 assorted prints and solids |
| R5A | 84 dark blue print 26 muslin |
| S1 | 224 assorted solids |
| T62 | 84 dk. blue print* |
| 2½" x 68" strip | 2 muslin |
| 2½" x 78" strip | 2 muslin |
| 4½" x 77" strip | 2 rose print |
| 4½" x 86" strip | 2 rose print |

*Reverse template for half the pieces.

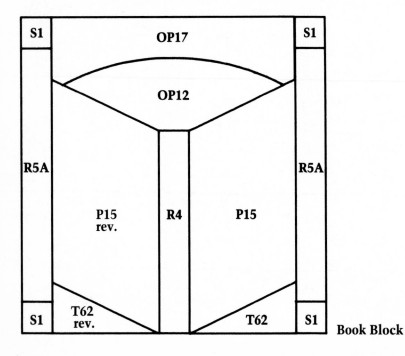

**Book Block**

**Quilt Construction:**

**1.** Following block diagram on page 14 for placement, make 42 blocks as follows: Join OP12 to OP17. Join T62 to P15 (book cover). Repeat with reversed T62 and reversed P15 pieces. Join book cover units to R4 (spine), stopping at top corner dots and backstitching. Join R4 to OP12, backstitching at each corner dot. Sew remaining angles outward on each side of R4. Join 1 S1 to each end of 1 dark blue R5A. Repeat for 1 more S1/R5A unit. Join 1 S1/R5A unit to each side of book block.

**2.** Set blocks together in 7 rows of 6 blocks across (see quilt diagram below). Join rows.

**3.** Attach 1 S1 to each end of 1 muslin R5A. Repeat 25 times for a total of 26 units. Join S1/R5A units end to end to form 2 rows of 6 and 2 rows of 7. Attach 1 (6-unit) row to top and 1 to bottom of quilt top. Join 1 remaining S1 piece to each end of each 7-unit row. Join 1 (7-unit) row to each side of quilt top.

**4.** Join 2½"-wide muslin inner borders to sides of quilt, mitering corners.

**5.** Join 4½"-wide rose print outer borders to sides of quilt, mitering corners.

**6.** Quilt as desired. Bind with dark blue print fabric.

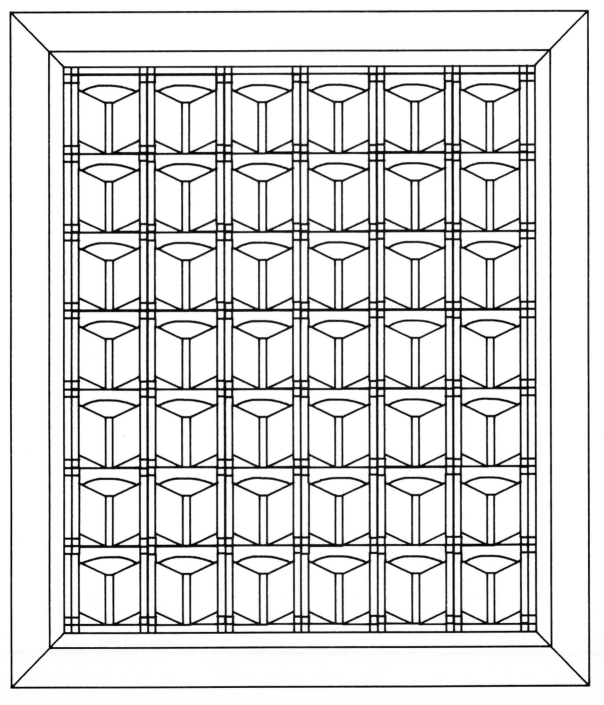

# Bed of Roses

Soft and sweet as an Indiana rosebud is this group quilt. The blocks are set on point to contrast with quilted muslin blocks. Many hands came together from the Quilters' Guild in Bloomington, Indiana, to stitch this magnificent raffle quilt. But it took just one hand to pull the winning ticket from the hat—mine!

Finished Size: 84" x 105"
Perimeter: 378"
Blocks: 20 (10⅝"-square) Rose blocks
30 (6" x 12") Rosebud Border blocks

## Fabric Requirements:

| | |
|---|---|
| Dk. green | 1½ yards |
| Dk. rose print | ¼ yard |
| Med. rose print | 5½ yards |
| Lt. rose print | ⅝ yard |
| Muslin | 6½ yards |
| Green print | 2⅝ yards |
| Backing | 6 yards |
| Dk. rose print for binding | ⅞ yard |

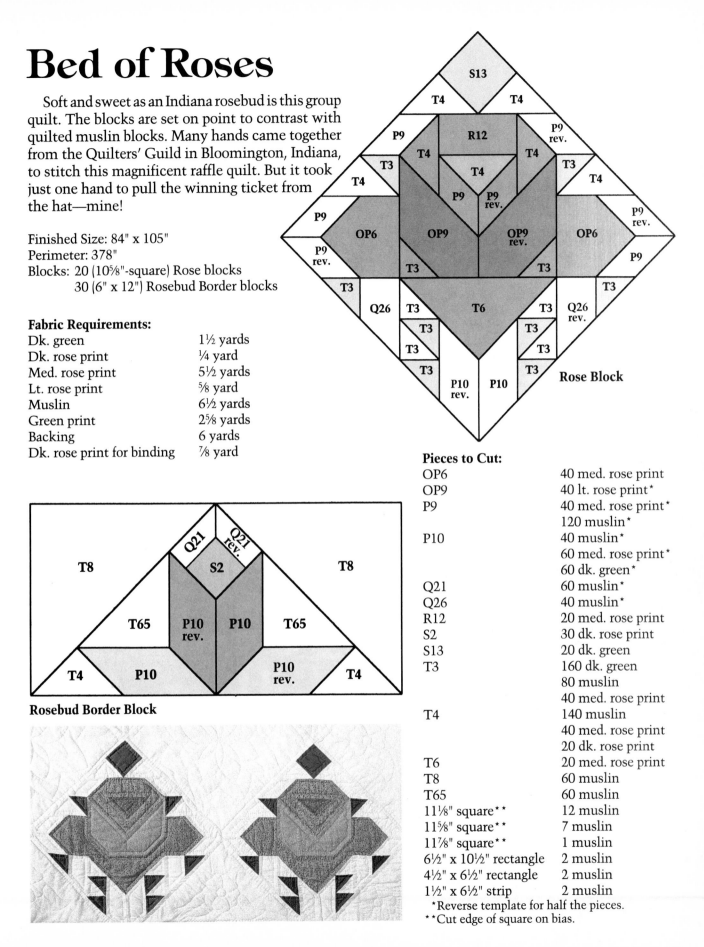

Rose Block

Rosebud Border Block

## Pieces to Cut:

| | |
|---|---|
| OP6 | 40 med. rose print |
| OP9 | 40 lt. rose print* |
| P9 | 40 med. rose print* |
| | 120 muslin* |
| P10 | 40 muslin* |
| | 60 med. rose print* |
| | 60 dk. green* |
| Q21 | 60 muslin* |
| Q26 | 40 muslin* |
| R12 | 20 med. rose print |
| S2 | 30 dk. rose print |
| S13 | 20 dk. green |
| T3 | 160 dk. green |
| | 80 muslin |
| | 40 med. rose print |
| T4 | 140 muslin |
| | 40 med. rose print |
| | 20 dk. rose print |
| T6 | 20 med. rose print |
| T8 | 60 muslin |
| T65 | 60 muslin |
| 11⅛" square** | 12 muslin |
| 11⅝" square** | 7 muslin |
| 11⅞" square** | 1 muslin |
| 6½" x 10½" rectangle | 2 muslin |
| 4½" x 6½" rectangle | 2 muslin |
| 1½" x 6½" strip | 2 muslin |

*Reverse template for half the pieces.
**Cut edge of square on bias.

## Quilt Construction:

**1.** Following block diagrams on page 17, make 20 rose blocks and 30 rosebud border blocks. Set aside.

**2.** Cut each of the 7 (11⅝") muslin squares in half diagonally to make 14 side triangles. Cut the 11⅞" muslin square into quarters diagonally to make 4 corner triangles.

**3.** Following quilt diagram below, set together rose blocks with 11⅛" muslin squares and side and corner triangles.

**4.** Following quilt diagram, join 5 rosebud border blocks to form bottom border. Cut 1 (2½" x 60½") strip from green print and join to bottom of unit. Cut 2 (2½" x 60½") strips from rose print and join to top and bottom of unit. Join border unit to bottom of quilt top. Cut 2 (2½" x 87½") strips from rose print and join to the sides of the quilt.

**5.** Join 7 rosebud border blocks to form right border. Join 1 (1½" x 6½") muslin strip to bottom edge of unit (see quilt diagram). Cut 1 (2½" x 85½") strip from green print and join to right edge of unit. Cut 1 (2½" x 8½") strip from rose print and join to bottom edge of unit. Repeat for left border, except join green print strip to left edge of unit. Join side borders to sides of quilt top.

**6.** For top border, make 1 row of 5 rosebud border blocks and 1 row of 6 rosebud border blocks. Join 1 (6½" x 10½") rectangle to each end of the 5-block row. Join 1 (4½" x 6½") rectangle to each end of the 6-block row. Join the 2 rows as shown in diagram. Cut 1 (2½" x 80½") strip from green print and join to bottom of unit. Cut 2 (2½" x 80½") rose print strips and join to top and bottom of unit. Join border unit to top of quilt top.

**7.** Follow quilt diagram to cut 2 (2½" x 105½") medium rose print strips and join to sides of quilt.

**8.** Quilt as desired. Bind with dark rose print fabric.

# Spotlight Dancing Spools

Quilter Thelma Caldwell sent me a roughly sketched graph for a Dancing Spools quilt. She requested that someone who knows about ballet improve it. For me, this meant a trip to the library to rediscover the dance positions. Each spool ballerina wears a net tutu and illustrates a different ballet stance. Appliquéd toe shoes and quilted legs accent the panel at center top.

**Block A Enlargement**

Finished Size: 34" x 56"
Perimeter: 180"
Blocks: 10 Ballerina blocks
        1 appliquéd panel

**Fabric Requirements:**

| | |
|---|---|
| Muslin | 1¾ yards |
| Dk. blue | 1¾ yards |
| Pink | ½ yard |
| Pink net | ¼ yard |
| Assorted scraps | ⅓ yard |
| Backing | 1¾ yards |
| Dk. blue for binding | ⅝ yard |
| Pink satin ribbon (¼"-wide) | 1 yard |

**Pieces to Cut*:**

| | |
|---|---|
| Q27 | 20 assorted |
| R1 | 2 muslin |
| S1 | 2 muslin |
| S4 | 10 assorted |
| T63 | 6 red |
| 4½" x 30¾" strip | 2 dk. blue |
| 3¾" x 73½" strip | 1 dk. blue |
| 1¼" x 8½" strip | 10 pink net |

*Refer to Step 1 to make templates for remaining pieces.

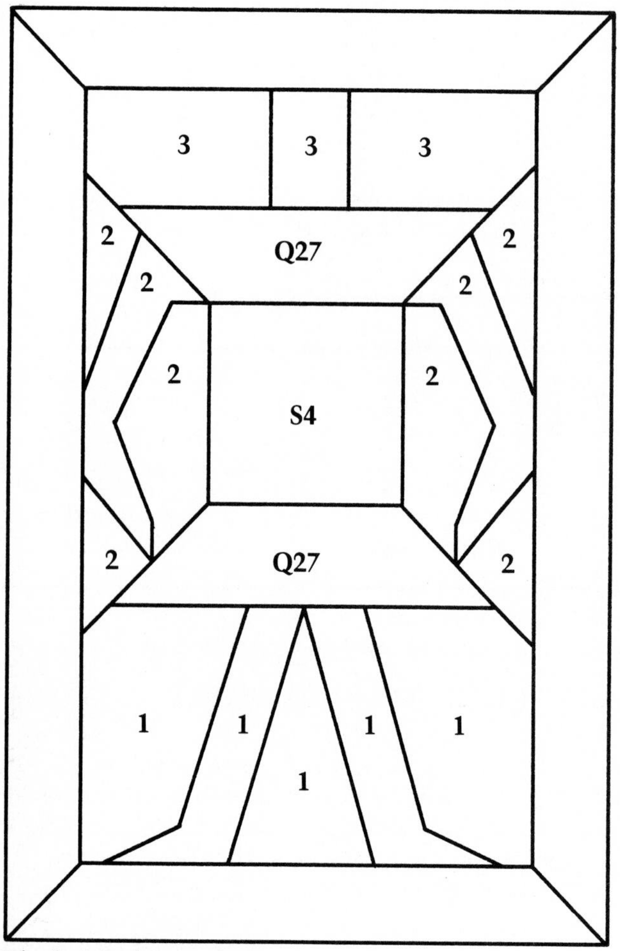

**Quilt Construction:**

**1.** Enlarge gridded blocks on page 125 onto gridded freezer paper. (Enlarge asymmetrical blocks C, H, and I onto shiny side of freezer paper.) Code templates in order of piecing (see Block A Enlargement). Color each numbered group of pieces a different color.

**2.** To cut and make blocks, refer to Gridded Freezer Paper as a Creative Tool, page 120. Gather net strips and baste to tops and sides of tutus. Appliqué shoes and ribbon ties onto rectangle at top center of quilt.

**3.** Refer to quilt diagram and photograph on page 21 to set blocks together with 1" mitered borders and solid rectangles to form 2 horizontal rows. Join horizontal rows.

**4.** Piece step sections and join to lower edges of side border strips. Join top, bottom, and side borders to quilt.

**5.** Hem 1 long edge of each 4½" x 30¾" side curtain strip. Gather all ends to a width of 3". Hem ends and 1 long edge of 3¾" x 73½" top curtain strip. Gather long raw edge to a width of 48½". With raw edges aligned and hemmed edges toward center, baste top and side curtains to outside edges of quilt borders (see photograph).

**6.** Stack backing, right side down; batting; and top, right side up. Quilt outlines of ballerinas' legs (see photograph and gridded pattern). Other quilting lines represent spotlight rays, radiating upward from behind each ballerina. Note seats and audience quilted on bottom border. Bind with dark blue fabric.

# Autumn Windows

Now you can save the vibrant colors of autumn leaves in cloth. Maple leaves from Maine became Alice Thomure's inspiration for this unusual quilt. Leaves are simply photocopied, transferred to freezer paper, and then cut from richly hued fabric. Appliqué the branches and leaves against white windows to suggest colorful fall foliage dancing in the crisp autumn air.

Alice chose to cross-hatch the solid squares in a double line of quilting, with straight lines behind the leaves. (The photograph below shows the bottom half of the quilt only.)

Finished Size: 102" x 102"
Perimeter: 408"
Blocks: 10 (18"-square) blocks with circles
11 (18"-square) plain blocks
2 (18" x 38") rectangles with ½" x 38" accent strips

**Fabric Requirements:**

| | |
|---|---|
| Navy | 8½ yards |
| White | 3⅞ yards |
| Red | ½ yard |
| Brown | 1 yard |
| Assorted scraps in autumn colors | 2 yards total |
| Backing | 9⅜ yards |
| Navy for binding | 1 yard |

**Pieces to Cut*:**

| | |
|---|---|
| 18½" square | 21 navy |
| 2½" x 18½" strip | 58 navy |
| 17½"-diameter circle | 10 white |
| 19½" x 40½" rectangle | 2 white |
| 1" x 38½" strip | 4 red |
| 2½" square | 36 red |

*Refer to Steps 1–2 to cut remaining pieces.

**Quilt Construction:**

1. Photocopy selected leaves to make templates for leaf appliqués. Trace templates onto dull side of freezer paper and cut out. Iron templates to right side of leaf fabrics and cut out, adding ½" seam allowance to each piece.

2. Cut lengths of brown fabric in desired shapes and sizes to represent tree limbs (see photograph).

3. Position leaf and limb appliqués on white circles and rectangles (see photograph). Stitch close to freezer paper around leaves and close to raw edge on limbs. Peel off freezer paper. Trim fabric as close to stitching line as possible.

4. Place a piece of lightweight paper under white fabric and outline each leaf and limb with narrow zigzag stitch, covering previous stitching line. Adjust width of zigzag stitch so that it narrows at leaf points. To stitch inside curves, lower needle into fabric on inside of stitching line, raise presser foot, pivot fabric, lower presser foot, and gently guide fabric as you stitch around curve. On outside curves, lower needle on outside of stitching line and proceed as above. Satin-stitch leaf stems as shown in photograph. Peel paper from behind fabric.

5. To reduce bulk in appliqués, trim away white fabric underneath each appliqué, leaving ¼" seam allowance all around.

6. Adding appliqués could cause the fabric to draw up a bit, and the cutting dimensions I have given allow for this. After adding appliqués, trim circles to measure 15½" in diameter and rectangles to measure 17½" x 38½". Join red accent strips to long edges of rectangles. Turn under seam allowances and hand-appliqué circles to navy squares. To reduce bulk, trim away navy fabric under circles, leaving ¼" seam allowance.

7. Join red accent squares to sashing strips to make horizontal rows of sashing (see quilt diagram). Following quilt diagram, set blocks and rectangles together with sashing.

8. Quilt as desired. Bind with navy fabric.

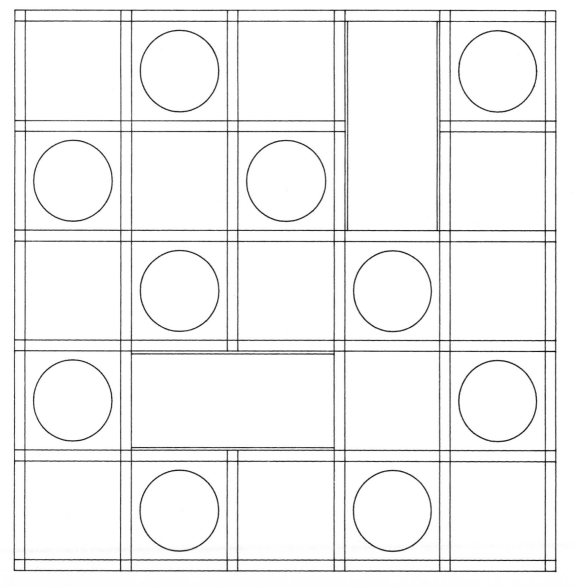

# Little Toot

Inspired by a colorful toy box, Marilyn Fluharty bright-
ened her grandson's room with this train quilt. Three rows
of trains, coming and going, span the top. Picture strip
piecing, based on a grid and sewn with freezer paper strips,
helps this project move along into the station quickly. Cut
fabric in duplicate with your rotary cutter in fast-forward
motion!

Finished Size: 60" x 105"
Perimeter: 330"
Blocks: 12 (12"-square) Car blocks
3 (12"-square) Engine blocks

**Fabric Requirements:**

| | |
|---|---|
| Blue | 2 yards |
| Red | 1¾ yards |
| Green | 1¾ yards |
| Yellow | ¼ yard |
| White | 2 yards |
| Ticking | 1¾ yards |
| Backing | 6½ yards |
| Red for binding | ⅞ yard |

**Pieces to Cut\*:**

| | |
|---|---|
| 10½" x 60½" strip | 1 blue |
| 15½" x 60½" strip | 1 blue, 1 red, 1 green |
| 2½" x 60½" strip | 3 ticking |
| 4½" x 60½" strip | 1 ticking, 1 blue |

*Refer to Step 2 to cut remaining pieces.

**Quilt Construction:**

**1.** Enlarge patterns on page 129 onto shiny sides of 2 (12") squares of gridded freezer paper.

**2.** Refer to Picture Strip Piecing, page 120, to cut and make blocks, following block diagrams below to join pieces. Refer to photograph for color placement, or place colors as desired.

**3.** Set blocks together in 3 rows as shown in quilt diagram.

**4.** Complete quilt top by joining train rows with colored strips of fabric as indicated in quilt diagram and photograph. Appliqué wheels to train cars as shown in diagrams.

**5.** Quilt as desired. Bind with red fabric.

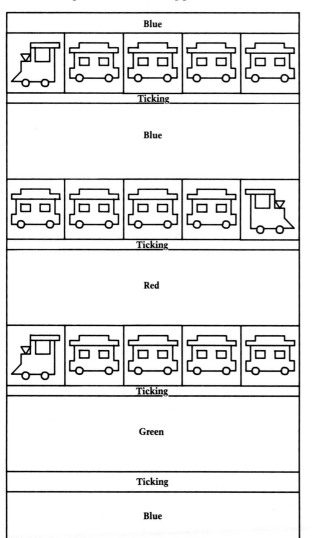

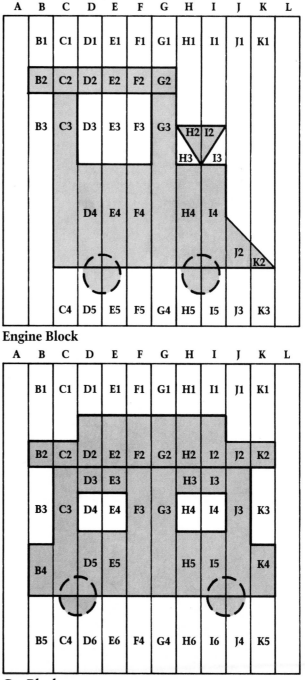

**Engine Block**

**Car Block**

# Hillside Village

The twenty houses in this quilt illustrate how using both the right and wrong sides of fabric can create a play of light and shadow. The side of the roof (template T1) and the side of the house (template P5) are cut from the reverse side of the fabric.

This design may look familiar to you. Its little sister, a 36-inch x 46-inch Hillside Village wall hanging, has already starred in my pattern club, *Spinning Spools*. For the full-sized quilt, I have increased the size of the block from 6 inches to 12 inches, added a window, and designed a new border.

Finished Size: 72" x 92"
Perimeter: 328"
Blocks: 20 (12"-square) blocks

**Fabric Requirements:**

| | |
|---|---|
| Assorted prints for houses | 1¾ yards total |
| White print | 1½ yards |
| Assorted black prints | 1 yard total |
| Lt. lavender print | 4½ yards |
| Dk. lavender print | ¾ yard |
| Dk. green print | 1¼ yards |
| Backing | 5¼ yards |
| Dk. green print for binding | ⅞ yard |

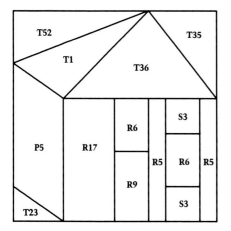

## Pieces to Cut:

| | |
|---|---|
| P5 | 20 house print */** |
| Q1 | 4 black print |
| R5 | 40 house print |
| R6 | 20 house print |
| | 20 white print |
| R9 | 20 white print |
| R17 | 20 house print |
| S3 | 40 house print |
| T1 | 20 black print */** |
| T19 | 37 white print |
| | 37 dk. lavender print |
| | 78 dk. green print |
| T23 | 20 lt. lavender print* |
| T35 | 20 lt. lavender print* |
| T36 | 20 black print* |
| T52 | 20 lt. lavender print* |
| 2½" x 12½" rectangle | |
| | 2 lt. lavender print |
| 4½" x 12½" rectangle | |
| | 5 lt. lavender print |
| 6½" x 12½" rectangle | |
| | 2 lt. lavender print |
| 8½" x 12½" rectangle | |
| | 5 lt. lavender print |
| 12½" square | 3 lt. lavender print |
| 12½" x 16½" rectangle | |
| | 3 lt. lavender print |
| 1½" x 64" inner border strip | |
| | 2 lt. lavender print |
| 1½" x 84" inner border strip | |
| | 2 lt. lavender print |
| 1½" x 66" inner border strip | |
| | 2 white print |
| 1½" x 86" inner border strip | |
| | 2 white print |

*Reverse template for half the pieces.
**Cut from reverse side of fabric.

## Quilt Construction:

**1.** Following block diagram (left) for placement, make 10 house blocks. Make 10 more house blocks, reversing order of pieces to make mirror images (see quilt diagram below).

**2.** Following quilt diagram, set blocks together with background pieces.

**3.** Add inner borders to quilt top, mitering corners (see photograph and quilt diagram).

**4.** To make top and bottom outer borders, join dark green, dark lavender, and white T19 border triangles, following quilt diagram and photograph for placement. Follow same procedure for 2 side borders, adding black corner Q1 pieces to ends. Join to quilt top.

**5.** Quilt as desired. Bind with dark green print fabric.

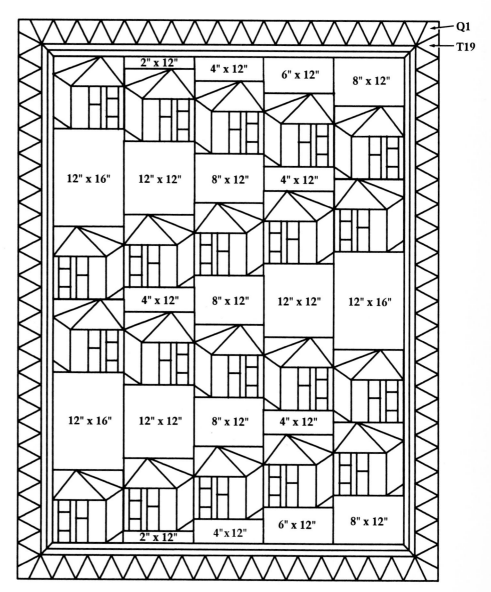

# GEOMETRIC GEMS

The following quilts were derived from popular and time-honored geometric shapes—but with a fresh approach.

*Grandma Evans's Chicken Feet*

Penny Wortman is a faithful contributor to the lap-quilting field. This scrap medley quilt, which Penny made from her Grandma Evans's leftovers, was lap-quilted. She added the Flying Geese border in sections to the perimeter blocks to be quilted along with the blocks.

Finished Size: 88" x 88"
Perimeter: 352"
Blocks: 25 (16"-square) blocks

## Fabric Requirements:

| | |
|---|---|
| Muslin | 6⅛ yards |
| Assorted pastel print scraps | 6⅛ yards |
| Backing | 8 yards |
| Muslin for binding | ⅞ yard |

## Pieces to Cut:

| | |
|---|---|
| P8 | 32 print* |
| P14 | 400 print* |
| R9 | 100 muslin |
| S1 | 16 muslin |
| S3 | 100 muslin |
| T10 | 16 muslin |
| T15 | 300 print |
| | 360 muslin |
| T46 | 320 print |
| 8½" square | 25 muslin |

*Reverse template for half the pieces.

## Quilt Construction:

1. Follow large block diagram to piece block as follows: Join 3 print T15 triangles. Repeat for 3 more T15 units. Attach 1 T15 unit to each side of center square and set aside.

Join 2 P14s and 2 reversed P14s to make corner stars. Repeat for 3 more corner stars. Set 2 muslin T15 triangles in each corner star as shown in diagram. Set 1 S3 corner square into each corner star unit. Join corner star units with 4 R9s. Join corner stars to center unit.

2. Using T46 and muslin T15 pieces, piece Flying Geese borders in 8-goose sections. (Note that geese change directions at center of each border strip.)
3. Following small block diagram, piece 4 corner blocks.
4. Following quilt diagram, join Flying Geese border sections and small corner blocks to perimeter blocks. Lap-quilt, using light green quilting thread. Join blocks to form rows. (See Lap-Quilting Connections, page 121.) Join rows. Bind with muslin.

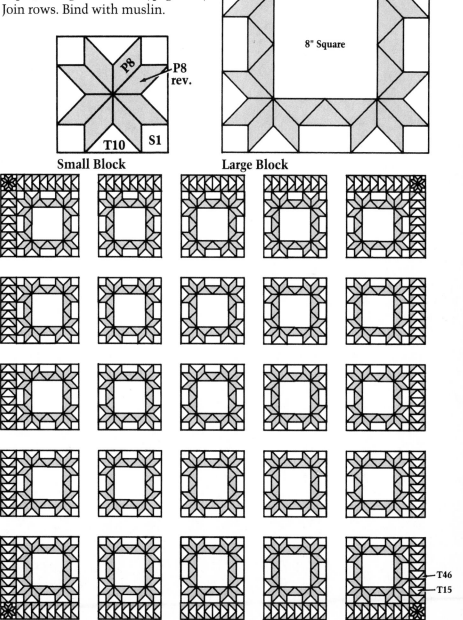

Small Block    Large Block

# Plaid Pinwheels

This quilt proves that plaids and checks *can* work in quilts. So don't be afraid to experiment. The simple, straightforward Pinwheel pattern makes this a great quilt on which to use a system of continuous machine-piecing.

Finished Size: 63" x 77"
Perimeter: 280"
Blocks: 99 (7"-square) Pinwheel blocks

**Fabric Requirements:**

| | |
|---|---|
| Assorted plaids and checks | 5⅛ yards total |
| Muslin | 2 yards |
| Backing | 4½ yards |
| Muslin for binding | ¾ yard |

**Pieces to Cut:**

| | |
|---|---|
| Q14 | 396 assorted plaids and checks |
| T32 | 396 muslin |

**Quilt Construction:**
**1.** Following quilt block diagram, piece 99 Pinwheel blocks as follows: Join T32 to Q14, aligning right angles of each piece.
**2.** Keep sewing in a continuous chain until 4 sets of matching checks and plaids are linked. Do not cut thread between pieces, but sew "on air" for a few stitches between pieces to create a "kite-tail" of triangles. Clip sections apart.
**3.** Align 2 matching triangles and join to form a larger triangle. Continue to join matching triangles in a continuous chain without cutting thread as in Step 2. Cut triangles apart, align matching triangles, and stitch to form square. As you sew, press seams in a clockwise direction around block.
**4.** Join blocks in 11 rows of 9 blocks each. Join rows.
**5.** Quilt with straight lines. Bind with muslin.

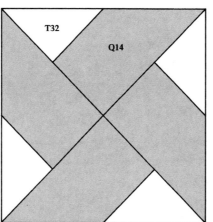

**Pinwheel Block**

# Star Glaze

A bold and beautiful print lends a new look to a classic Virginia Reel setting that, like *Ocean Blue* on page 38, uses the Monkey Wrench block. Try your hand at this tried-and-true block, which is made mostly of triangles surrounding a simple four-patch.

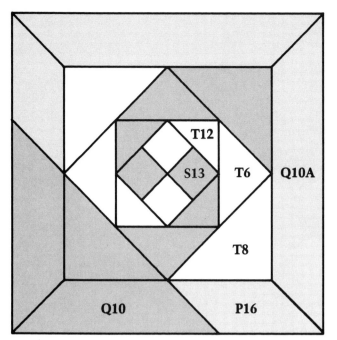

**Monkey Wrench Block**

Finished Size: 54" x 54"
Perimeter: 216"
Blocks: 4 (18"-square) Monkey
          Wrench blocks

**Fabric Requirements:**

| | |
|---|---|
| Large green-and-purple print | 1¾ yards |
| Purple | 2 yards |
| Small green print | 1½ yards |
| Backing | 3¼ yards |
| Purple for binding | ¾ yard |

**Pieces to Cut:**

| | |
|---|---|
| P16 | 8 small green print |
| Q10 | 8 purple |
| Q10A | 8 small green print |
| S13 | 8 large print |
| | 8 purple |
| T6 | 8 large print |
| | 8 purple |
| T8 | 8 large print |
| | 8 purple |
| T12 | 8 large print |
| | 8 purple |
| 18½" square | 4 large print |
| | 1 purple |

**Quilt Construction:**

**1.** Following block diagram at left and quilt photograph for placement, piece 4 Monkey Wrench blocks with borders.

**2.** Machine-quilt corner blocks, following fabric design. Hand-quilt center block and pieced blocks.

**3.** Join quilted blocks in 3 rows of 3 blocks each. (See Backing Accents, page 122.) Join rows. Bind with purple fabric.

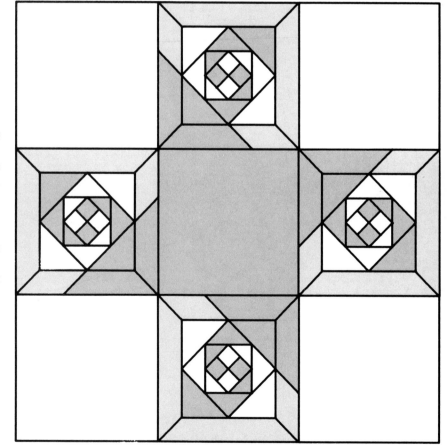

# Copycat

Cut, stitch, and shift. It's that simple for a quilt that's the "cat's meow."

Finished Size: 39" x 65"
Perimeter: 208"

**Fabric Requirements:**

| | |
|---|---|
| Beige print | 2¾ yards |
| Dk. blue print | ¾ yard |
| Lavender | ¾ yard |
| Med. blue print | ¾ yard |
| Backing | 2 yards |

**Pieces to Cut:**

| | |
|---|---|
| R13 | 3 beige print |
| | 2 dk. blue print |
| | 2 med. blue print |
| | 2 lavender |
| T17 | 6 beige print |
| | 1 dk. blue print |
| | 1 med. blue print |
| | 1 lavender |
| T41 | 3 beige print |
| | 2 dk. blue print |
| | 2 med. blue print |
| | 2 lavender |
| T49 | 3 beige print |
| | 3 dk. blue |
| | 3 med. blue |
| | 3 lavender |
| T49 reversed | 9 beige print |
| | 2 dk. blue |
| | 2 med. blue |
| | 2 lavender |
| 3½" x 15½" strip | 2 beige print |
| 3½" x 65½" strip | 2 beige print |

## Quilt Construction:

1. With right sides up, layer ¾ yard of beige print and next 3 fabrics, matching selvages. Cut 3 (5½"-wide) strips across fabrics through all layers.

2. Join strips along long edges in order listed in Fabric Requirements to make 12 rows, repeating the 4 colors in the same order each time (see Diagram 1). Press seam allowances to 1 side, alternating seam directions across strips.

3. Cut across seam lines of pieced fabric and make 11 (3½"-wide) strips.

4. Reposition strips to form chevron shape as shown in Diagram 2. Using seam ripper, separate rows as shown in Diagram 3. Remove center group of rectangles. Reposition sections as shown in Diagram 4, moving bottom section of strips to top, and join. Set aside.

5. Following Copycat Strips diagram on page 37 for placement, piece vertical Copycat strips. Position all vertical strips as shown in Diagram 5. Join strip sections vertically to form 11 long strips. Join strips horizontally. Join 65½" border strips to each side of pieced strips.

6. Quilt as follows: Cut a 43" x 69" piece each from backing and batting. Layer batting and backing. With wrong sides facing, align center strip of quilt top with center of backing and batting. Fold half of the top back to reveal center seam allowance. Pin in place. Stitch down previously sewn seam through all layers, using bobbin thread to match backing and a walking foot. Fold center forward. Pin center panel through all layers. Continue stitching until all 6 seam allowances are secured. Repeat on other side of quilt, joining 5 remaining pieced strips and border strip.

7. Add buttons or embroidered eyes and ribbon whiskers to cats. Trim excess batting even with top. Trim backing, leaving 1" extension all around. Fold backing to front of quilt, turn under raw edge, and secure with a wide zigzag stitch.

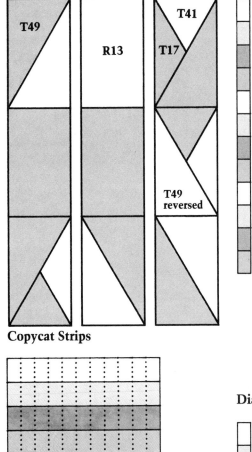

**T49**  **R13**  **T41**  **T17**  **T49 reversed**

**Copycat Strips**

**Diagram 1**

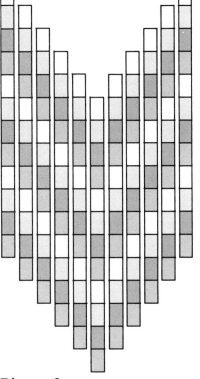

**Diagram 2**

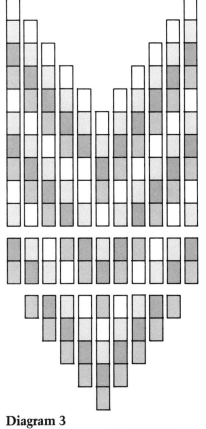

**Diagram 3**

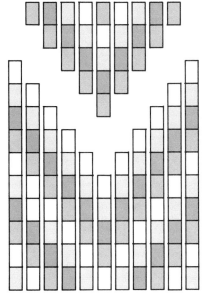

**Diagram 4**

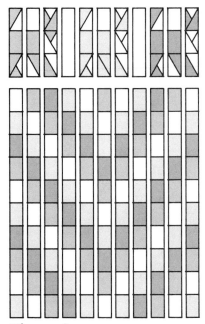

**Diagram 5**

# A Quilt Pattern
## and Instructions by Yours Truly
# The Yours Truly Virginia Reel
## Quick Quilt and coordinating pillow
### Introduced in the April, 1979 Woman's Day Magazine

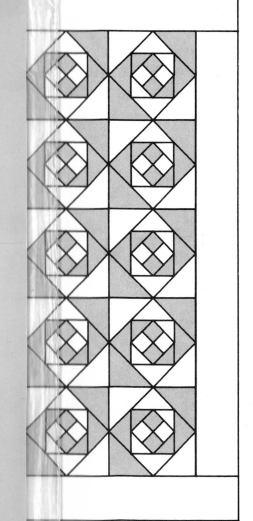

**Contents: Patterns and instructions for quilt
in three sizes and coordinating pillow**

Yours Truly, Inc./Box 80218/Atlanta, Ga. 30366/ © Made and Printed in USA
Product No. 3917                          Form No. 726-0381

# The Ultimate Postage Stamp Quilt

It's just a collection of one-inch squares—but with special color planning, it became a gem. I designed this quilt and then coerced my friends in the Western North Carolina Quilters Guild into piecing it. It was raffled at the guild's annual fall quilt show. Oh, to have been the lucky winner!

Finished Size: 89" x 115"
Perimeter: 408"
Blocks: 12 (25"-square) Postage Stamp blocks

## Fabric Requirements:

| | |
|---|---|
| Assorted scraps | 12 yards total |
| Navy | 3⅛ yards |
| Muslin | 2⅛ yards |
| Backing | 10 yards |
| Navy for binding | 1 yard |

## Pieces to Cut:

| | |
|---|---|
| S1 | 5,124 from assorted scraps |
| | 62 navy |
| | 62 muslin |
| 1½" x 45" strip | 27 navy |
| | 27 muslin |
| 1½" x 72" strip | 2 navy |
| 1½" x 3½" strip | 48 assorted prints |
| 1½" x 5½" strip | 48 assorted prints |
| 1½" x 7½" strip | 48 assorted prints |
| 1½" x 9½" strip | 48 assorted prints |
| 1½" x 11½" strip | 48 assorted prints |
| 1½" x 13½" strip | 31 assorted prints |
| 3½" x 5½" strip | 4 navy |
| 3½" x 26½" strip | 6 navy |
| 3½" x 27½" strip | 4 navy |
| 3½" x 28½" strip | 4 navy |
| 1½" x 26½" strip | 6 muslin |
| 1½" x 27½" strip | 4 muslin |
| 1½" x 28½" strip | 4 muslin |

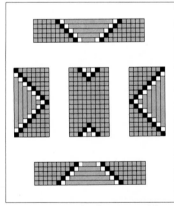

**Diagram 1: Block Assembly**

## Quilt Construction:

1. To make this quilt, you will need 12 Postage Stamp blocks. Study the quilt photograph to arrange the colors in each block of the quilt. There are 4 blocks shaded from blue to red at the corners of the quilt; 2 blocks shaded from rust to red to orange at center top and center bottom; 4 blocks shaded from blue to green at sides; and 2 blocks shaded from gold to pale yellow in the center.

2. For each block, you will need 373 S1 pieces from assorted solids and prints in the proper colors and 1½"-wide strips in colors to coordinate with squares (refer to Diagram 1 for number and placement of strips).

3. Join 1 (1½" x 45") navy strip to 1 (1½" x 45") muslin strip along long edges. Cut across this strip at 1½" intervals to make 30 (2-square) units. Repeat to make 52 (2-square) units per block and 62 units for sashing. Cut across 2 (1½" x 72") navy strips at 1½" intervals to make 96 squares for all 12 blocks. (Eight navy squares will be used for each block.)

4. Make a piecing guide for each block by drawing a 25" square on a piece of paper and marking it with a 1" grid. On grid, lay out colors as desired, pinning each square of fabric to a square on grid. Add strips, navy squares, and 2-square units, referring to Diagram 1 for positions.

5. To assemble block, starting on outside and working inward, unpin and join squares, 2-square units, and strips to make 5 rectangles as shown in Diagram 1. Join rectangles to complete block. Make 12 blocks.

6. Referring to Diagram 2 for number and placement of pieces, make 4 vertical sashing strips and 1 horizontal sashing strip. Repeat 3 more times for 4 rows. Make 2 side border units as shown. Repeat 2 more times for 3 rows. Make 2 side border units for Row 4, as shown in Diagram 3.

7. To assemble Row 1, join 3 blocks and 4 vertical sashing strips as shown in Diagram 2. Join horizontal sashing strip to top of row. Add side border units. Repeat for Rows 2–3.

8. Make 1 more horizontal sashing strip and join it and remaining strip to the top and bottom edges of Row 4. Join side border units. Assemble top and bottom borders as shown in Diagram 3. Join the top border to Row 1 and the bottom border to Row 4.

9. Layer each row with batting and backing. Lap-quilt as desired. Join rows (see Lap-Quilting Connections, page 121). Bind edges with navy fabric to complete quilt.

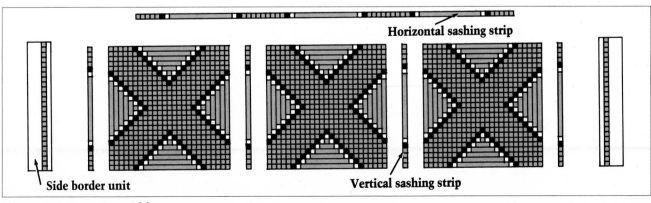

**Diagram 2: Row Assembly**

Side border unit

Horizontal sashing strip

Vertical sashing strip

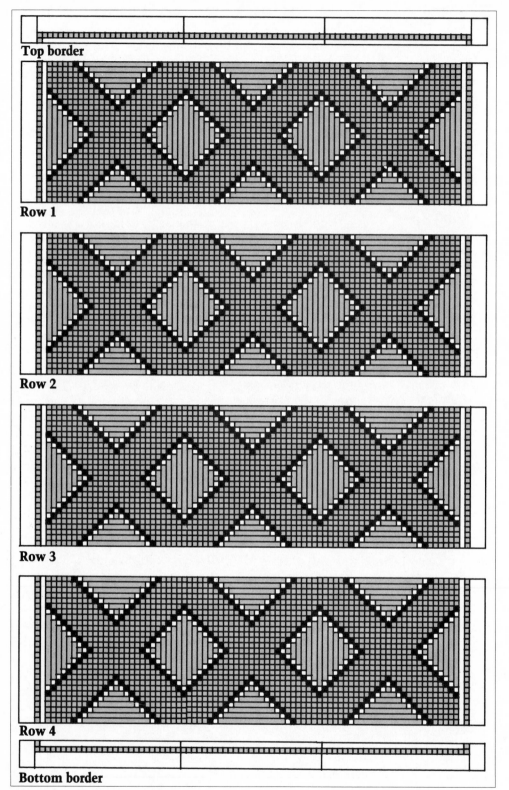

**Top border**

**Row 1**

**Row 2**

**Row 3**

**Row 4**

**Bottom border**

**Diagram 3: Quilt Assembly**

# Postage Stamp Pillow

Inch by inch, anything is a cinch. Start with one basic block from *The Ultimate Postage Stamp* quilt on page 40. Add borders, backing, zipper, and pillow form for a great throw pillow.

Finished size: 33" square

**Material Requirements:**

Assorted scraps 1¼ yards total
Muslin 2 yards
Navy 2 yards
22" zipper
25"-square pillow form

**Pieces to Cut:**

| | |
|---|---|
| S1 | 485 assorted scraps |
| | 8 navy |
| 1½" x 3½" strip | 4 assorted scraps |
| 1½" x 5½" strip | 4 assorted scraps |
| 1½" x 7½" strip | 4 assorted scraps |
| 1½" x 9½" strip | 4 assorted scraps |
| 1½" x 11½" strip | 4 assorted scraps |
| 1½" x 45" strip | 2 navy |
| | 2 muslin |
| 1½" x 25½" strip | 2 muslin |
| 1½" x 27½" strip | 2 muslin |
| 2½" x 29½" strip | 2 navy |
| 2½" x 33½" strip | 2 navy |
| 33½" square | 2 muslin |
| | 1 navy |

**Pillow Construction:**

1. Follow Steps 2–5 on page 41 to make 1 Postage Stamp block.
2. Join 1½" x 25½" muslin strips to 2 opposite sides of block. Join 1½" x 27½" muslin strips to other sides.
3. From remaining S1 pieces, make 2 (27½") strips and 2 (29½") strips. Join 27½" strips to 2 opposite sides of block. Join 29½" strips to remaining sides.
4. Join 2½" x 29½" navy strips to 2 opposite sides of block. Join 2½" x 33½" navy strips to remaining sides.
5. To line block, with right sides facing and using ¼" seam, sew block to 1 (33½") muslin square, leaving 5" opening on 1 side for turning. Turn, press, and slipstitch opening closed. Topstitch close to edge around block.
6. To line pillow back, with right sides facing and using ¼" seam, sew remaining 33½" muslin square to 33½" navy square, leaving 5" opening on 1 side for turning.

Turn, press, and slipstitch opening closed. Topstitch close to edges around back.

7. Align pillow front and back, with lining sides facing. With front up, pin through all layers at 2 adjacent corners, on seam line between muslin border and pieced center.
8. Insert zipper on one side opening, 4" from edge. Stitch half the zipper on back lining and other half on front lining. Stitch in-the-ditch next to the muslin border and 25" square. Stitch remaining 3 sides of pillow in same ditch seam to connect 2 sections.
9. Insert pillow form.

# VACATION QUILTS

Keep those design juices flowing—even when relaxing on vacation. New ideas are around every bend in the road.

*Masks, Moose, and Qupak*

# Masks, Moose, and Qupak

The opportunity to travel in Alaska, teaching and taping for the PBS-TV *Lap Quilting* series, has left an indelible impression on me. This quilt, based on my Alaskan experiences, depicts the masks I discovered at the University of Alaska in Fairbanks, the moose I saw minutes after my plane landed, and the qupak technique I learned from Etta Lord.

(Qupak is a decorative trim once made from calf skin and attached to the edges of parkas. Today, single-fold bias tape replaces the calf skin.)

The three Alaskan motifs come together in this strip quilt. Print fabric found in, of all places, the Caribbean islands adds festive flair and charm to the patchwork.

Finished Size: 82" x 102"
Perimeter: 368"
Blocks: 4 (8"-square) Mask blocks
      2 (10"-square) Mask blocks
      1 (14"-square) Mask block

## Fabric Requirements:

| | |
|---|---|
| Assorted prints | 5 yards total |
| White | 2½ yards |
| Burgundy | 2½ yards |
| Gold | ⅛ yard |
| Backing | 6¼ yards |
| Print for binding | ⅞ yard |

## Pieces to Cut:

**8" Mask Blocks**

| | |
|---|---|
| OP26 | 8 white |
| OP26A | 4 white |
| OP26B | 12 white |
| OP28 | 16 print |
| OP28A | 12 print |
| S3 | 8 white |
| S5 | 4 print |
| T71 | 8 contrasting print |

**10" Mask Blocks**

| | |
|---|---|
| OP2 | 8 print |
| OP2A | 4 print |
| OP3 | 8 white |
| OP3A | 2 white |
| P18 | 4 gold |
| S4 | 8 white |
| S15 | 2 print |

**14" Mask Block**

| | |
|---|---|
| OP27 | 8 white |
| OP27A | 1 white |
| OP27B | 1 white |
| OP29 | 10 print |
| OP29A | 1 print |
| P19 | 2 gold |
| S16 | 1 print |

**Totem Bodies**

| | |
|---|---|
| P2 | 16 print |
| P17 | 18 print |
| Q9 | 13 print |
| Q11 | 66 print |
| S18 | 20 white |
| T33 | 40 print |
| | 4 burgundy |
| T48 | 26 white* |
| T51 | 32 white |
| T64 | 132 white |
| T66 | 36 burgundy |
| 5" x 10½" rectangle | 2 white |
| 2½" x 8½" rectangle | 2 white |
| 4½" x 14½" rectangle | 1 white |
| 4½" x 8½" rectangle | 4 white |
| 8½" x 14½" rectangle | 1 white |

**Borders**

| | |
|---|---|
| Moose appliqué | 5 burgundy |
| | 5 white |

*Reverse template for half the pieces.

| | |
|---|---|
| 8½" x 82½" strip | 1 burgundy |
| | 1 white |
| 3½" x 82½" strip | 1 print |
| 5½" x 82½" strip | 1 white |
| 3½" x 78½" strip | 2 print |
| 5½" x 78½" strip | 2 white |

## Quilt Construction:

**1.** Following mask block diagrams, make 2 each (8"), 2 (10"), and 1 (14") mask blocks. Machine-appliqué eyes in place. Add purchased rickrack for mouths and beads and buttons for noses and earrings (see photograph).

**2.** Follow quilt diagram on page 48 to make totem bodies and join them to their respective mask blocks. Join totem bodies, following quilt diagram, to complete totem unit.

**3.** Attach 1 (4½" x 78½") print strip to opposite sides of totem unit.

**4.** Following quilt diagram, appliqué 5 white moose to 8½" x 82½" burgundy strip; appliqué 5 burgundy moose to 8½" x 82½" white strip. Join moose strips. Join moose unit to bottom of totem unit.

**5.** Join 4½" x 82½" print strip to bottom of moose unit.

**6.** See Qupak Border Construction on page 49 to make 2 (4½" x 78½") and 1 (4½" x 82½") qupak borders.

**7.** Following quilt diagram, join qupak borders to sides and bottom of quilt.

**8.** Stack backing, right side down; high-loft batting; and top, right side up. Baste. Hand-quilt around masks and moose as in photograph. Using transparent thread, quilt in-the-ditch along the long vertical seams. (Before machine-quilting, roll the quilt tightly and secure with bicycle clips.

Unroll as you quilt.) Following the photograph, add tie-tacking as final accent, attaching 1 tiny bead to each tie and securing with a double square knot. Bind with print fabric.

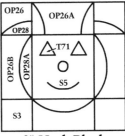

**8" Mask Block**

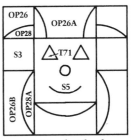

**8" Mask Block**

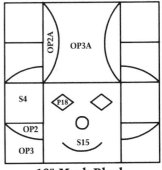

**10" Mask Block**

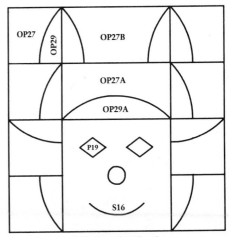

**14" Mask Block**

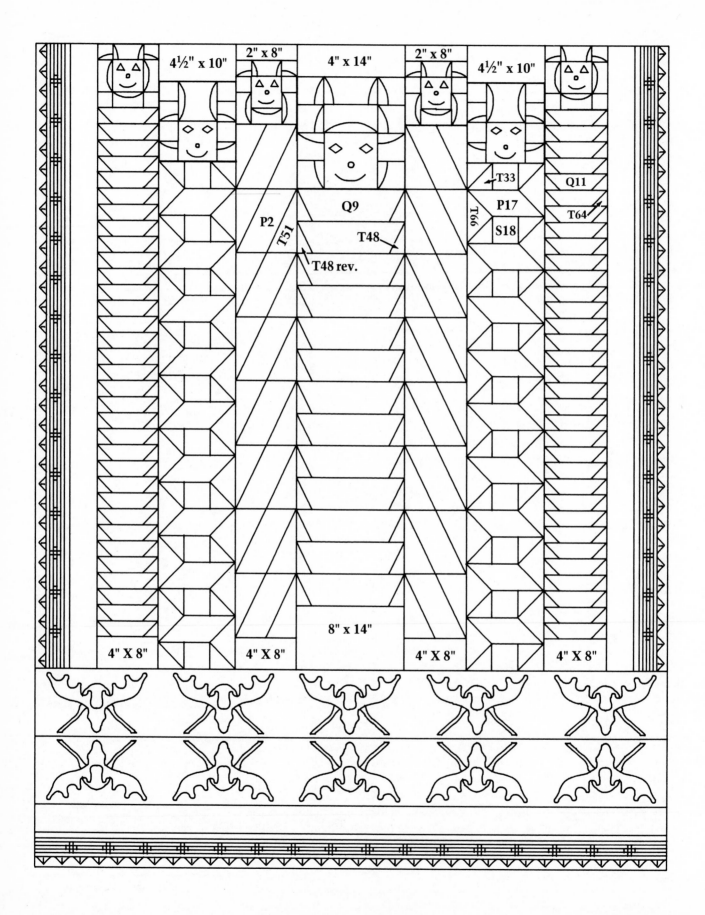

4½" x 10"  2" x 8"  4" x 14"  2" x 8"  4½" x 10"

T33  Q11

Q9  P17

P2  T51  T48  S18  T64

T48 rev.

8" x 14"

4" X 8"  4" X 8"  4" X 8"  4" X 8"  4" X 8"

## Qupak Border Construction:

**1.** To make qupak borders, you will need the following amounts of single-fold bias tape (either purchased or handmade) in colors of your choice: 16½ yards (1"-wide) for Row 1 "rickrack" edging; 6¾ yards (⅞"-wide) each for Rows 2–6; and 5½ yards (⅞"-wide) for cross strips.

**2.** To make bottom border, use 4½" x 82½" white strip for foundation fabric. (Use 4½" x 78½" white strips to make side borders.) Mark straight lines across foundation 2" from outside edge of border, 1" apart, as sewing guide. Also mark midpoints, 2½" apart, between these lines (see Diagram 1). This will be the placement line for "rickrack" edging.

**3.** For Row 1, refer to Diagram 1. To make points of "rickrack" trim, with 1"-wide bias tape (plaid "rickrack" in photograph), position tape as shown and edgestitch point-to-point. With needle down at placement line, clip bias tape on top edges as shown in diagram to release fabric to make next point. Continue in same manner, placing points an equal distance apart across width of foundation fabric (see quilt diagram and photograph).

**4.** Using ⅞"-wide bias tape, position bottom edge of tape so that it just overlaps top edge of "rickrack." Fold tucks in "rickrack" points in same direction (see Diagram 2). Edgestitch bottom edge of tape in place to complete Row 2.

**5.** Using another color of ⅞"-wide bias tape, position this strip across top edge of first strip ½" above stitching line for first strip for Row 3. To make cross strips, insert 1"-long (½"-wide) bias strips of contrasting color under tape between points and stitch (see Diagram 3). See photograph and quilt diagram for placement of these cross strips.

**6.** Complete Row 4 in same manner as Row 3. As you sew, flip back each cross strip from previous row and insert 1 new cross strip on each side (see Diagram 4).

**7.** Complete Row 5 in same manner as Row 3. As you sew, flip back each pair of cross strips from previous row and insert another cross strip in between, opposite the cross strip on Row 2 (see Diagram 5).

**8.** Complete Row 6, flipping back each cross strip from previous row. Edgestitch top of Row 6 bias strip to foundation fabric. (See Diagram 6 for finished qupak border.)

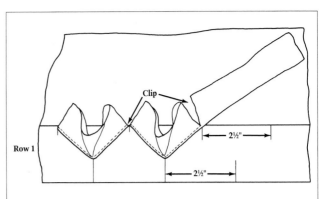

**Diagram 1**

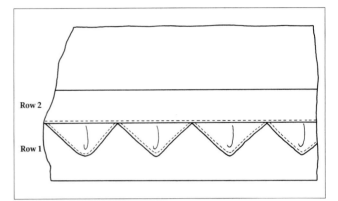

**Diagram 2**

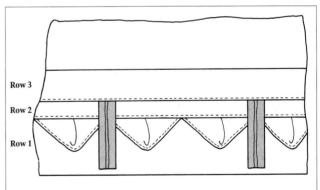

**Diagram 3**

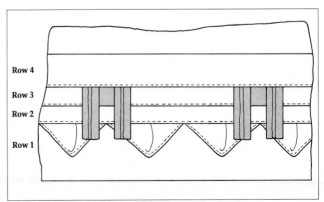

**Diagram 4**

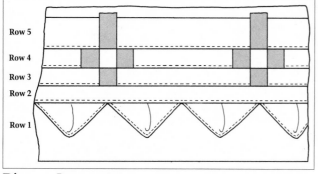

**Diagram 5**

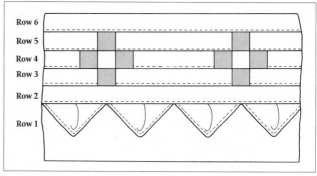

**Diagram 6**

# Qupak Workshirt

The qupak technique is great for adding accents to smaller projects such as totes, vests, and skirts. Here, I've used it to embellish a chambray workshirt.

**Material Requirements:**
Chambray workshirt with 2 breast pockets
5⅝ yards (1"-wide) single-fold lavender bias tape
1⅜ yards (1"-wide) single-fold turquoise bias tape
1⅞ yards (1"-wide) single-fold navy bias tape
3 yards (1"-wide) single-fold white bias tape

**Shirt Construction:**
**1.** Using seam ripper, carefully remove pockets from shirt and set aside.
**2.** Trim 2" from bottom of shirt. Reserve trimmed fabric.
**3.** Using seam ripper, carefully separate shoulder seams of shirt.
**4.** Cut lavender tape into 8 (17½") strips for shirt front, 8 (6") strips for pockets, and 2 (6") strips for bottom front of shirt. Cut turquoise tape into 2 (17½") strips for shirt front and 2 (6") strips for pockets. Cut navy tape into 64 (1") pieces. Cut white tape into 2 (17½") strips for shirt front, 2 (28") strips for "rickrack" on shirt front, and 2 (8") strips for "rickrack" on pockets.
**5.** See Qupak Border Construction, page 49, to sew qupak trim on front of shirt and pockets, using the shirt as foundation fabric. Place "rickrack" points 1½" from edges of shirt. Substitute bias tape measurements in Step 3 above for measurements in Qupak Border Construction. Add Row 7 of 17½" white bias strips to complete qupak trim.

**6.** Join shoulder seams.
**7.** Edgestitch 2 (6") lavender bias tape strips across bottom front of shirt on each side, covering ends of qupak trim and turning under raw edges at ends of tape.
**8.** Turn under bottom of shirt 1½" from cut edge and press. Turn under a narrow hem along cut edge and press to form drawstring casing. Edgestitch in place.
**9.** Edgestitch pockets in place on sleeves as shown in photograph.
**10.** Using reserved fabric, cut and piece a drawstring ½" wide and 36" longer than length around bottom of shirt. Insert drawstring in casing.

# Cruise and Quilt Banner

This wall hanging was designed on gridded freezer paper so that the drawn lines become the outlines of the templates. Feel free to add a new star, change the angle of the sun, or spell the name of your ship using the nautical alphabet. The flags here spell the name of the ship that sailed us on a memorable quilting cruise—*Caribe*.

Finished Size: 27" x 32"
Perimeter: 118"
Blocks: 1 (24" x 27") ship panel
       1 (8" x 27") fish panel

## Fabric Requirements:

| | |
|---|---|
| Navy print | ⅝ yard |
| White | ¼ yard |
| Med. blue print | ⅞ yard |
| Yellow print | ⅛ yard |
| Red print | ⅛ yard |
| Green print | ¼ yard |
| Rose print | ¼ yard |
| Multicolor print | ¼ yard |
| Backing | 1 yard |
| Assorted scraps from above fabrics for binding | ½ yard total |

## Pieces to Cut*:

| | |
|---|---|
| Q17 (with notch) | 4 multicolor print |
| Q17 (without notch) | 6 rose print |
| | 6 green print |
| | 2 multicolor print |
| T39 | 4 rose print |
| | 4 green print |
| T54 | 18 med. blue print |

*Refer to Step 3 to make templates for remaining pieces.

## Quilt Construction:

**1.** Following quilt diagram at right, make fish panel.
**2.** To make fish noses that extend from quilt, with right sides facing and raw edges aligned, sew 2 green print T39 pieces together, leaving 1 end open as shown on pattern. Trim seam, turn, and press. Repeat with 2 rose print T39 pieces. With raw edges aligned, sew green print nose to green print fish on right edge of fish panel; sew rose print nose to rose print fish on left edge of fish panel.
**3.** Enlarge ship panel pattern on page 127 onto the shiny side of a 24" x 27" piece of gridded freezer paper. (Join lengths of freezer paper to get the correct width by overlapping edges and pressing with warm iron.)

**4.** Refer to Picture Strip Piecing, page 120, to code freezer paper templates, cut pieces, join strips, and make panel. Refer to photograph for color placement. (*Note:* Pieces outlined with broken lines are to be cut and appliquéd to the finished panel.)
**5.** Join ship panel to fish panel.
**6.** Quilt as desired. Piece bias strips of print fabric as shown in photograph and bind edges of quilt. Press extended fish noses toward edge of quilt and tack to binding. Make and attach a casing to back of banner for hanging.

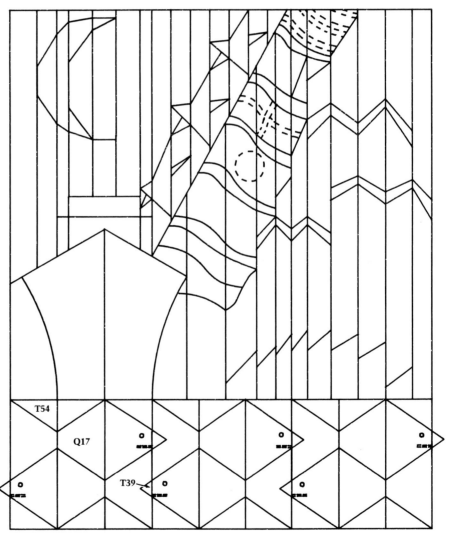

# The Big Ship

This quilt is a patchwork souvenir of one of my quilting cruises.

Finished Size: 60" x 60"
Perimeter: 240"
Blocks: 1 (6"-square) Split Star block
        4 (12"-square) Sail blocks

## Fabric Requirements*:

| | |
|---|---|
| White | 1⅜ yards |
| Multicolor print | ½ yard |
| Aqua | 1½ yards |
| Yellow | 1½ yards |
| Pink | 1½ yards |
| Backing | 3½ yards |
| Scraps from above fabrics for binding | ¾ yard total |

*Yardage for pieced sails not included.

## Pieces to Cut**:

| | |
|---|---|
| Q16 | 4 yellow |
| S10 | 1 multicolor print |
| T20 | 4 pink |
| T21 | 4 aqua |
| T34 | 8 white*** |
| 12½" square | 7 white |
| | 2 multicolor print |
| 12⅞" square | 3 white |
| | 1 multicolor print |
| 6½" square | 4 white |
| | 4 multicolor print |

**Cutting instructions for pieced sails not included. See Step 6 for instructions for cutting wavy borders.
***Reverse template for half the pieces.

## Quilt Construction:

**1.** Cut 12⅞" squares in half diagonally to make 6 white triangles and 2 multicolor print triangles. Set aside.
**2.** Create 4 sails to fit 1 diagonal half of a 12⅞" square. (If you prefer, cut sails from print fabric.) Join sails to 4 white triangles to make 4 sail blocks.
**3.** Following block diagram above, piece Split Star.
**4.** On 1 white 6½" square, measure 4¾" in from 1 corner along raw edge

and mark. Measure 4¾" in from same corner on adjacent side. With straightedge, draw line connecting these 2 points. Cut off corner along drawn line and discard. Repeat with 3 remaining white squares. Follow quilt diagram at bottom of page to

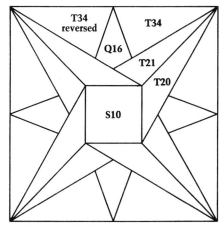

**Split Star Block**

join these 4 pieces to Split Star block.
**5.** Follow quilt diagram and photograph to set all blocks and triangles together.
**6.** To create wavy border, refer to Making Curved Templates, page 120, and make 4 (6½" x 48½") pieced border strips, referring to quilt diagram and photograph for suggested shapes and color placement.
**7.** Join a border to top and bottom of quilt. Join 6½" multicolor print squares to ends of remaining borders. Join borders to sides of quilt.
**8.** Quilt letters N, S, E, and W around compass points (see photograph). Radiating lines from sun sail are quilted with metallic thread. The students' names are stitched on waves underneath ship. Piece bias strips of fabric as shown in photograph and bind edges of quilt.

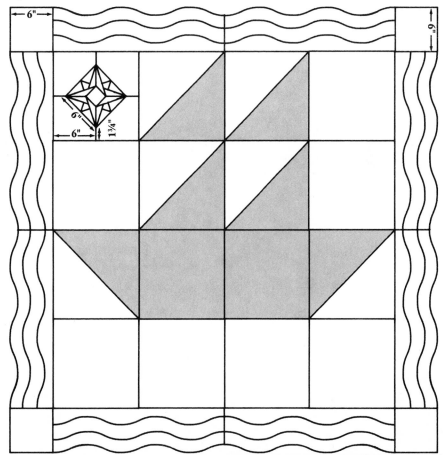

# Moonbeams Over Many Ports

A quilter on vacation has a special mission while scouting tourist shops—finding fabric, of course. It's a universal search and the inspiration for many a new quilt. My special background fabric used in this quilt was a real find on Grand Cayman. It is complete with the British flag, pirates, fish, and a map of the island.

Finished Size: 65½" x 78½"
Perimeter: 288"
Blocks:  8 (12"-square) Cruisin' blocks
        8 (12"-square) Moonbeam blocks
        15 (4½"-square) Mini-Cruisin' blocks

## Fabric Requirements:

| | |
|---|---|
| Assorted blue print | 3 yards total |
| Black | 1 yard |
| White | 1 yard |
| Red | ¾ yard |
| Yellow | Scrap |
| Green | ¾ yard |
| Vacation print | 2 yards |
| Backing | 4½ yards |
| Black for binding | ¾ yard |

## Pieces to Cut*:

| | |
|---|---|
| OP10 | 16 blue print** |
| OP30 | 8 black |
| OP30 reversed | 8 white |
| OP31 | 16 blue print** |
| Q3 | 8 white |
| Q3 reversed | 8 black |
| Q4 | 16 blue print** |
| Q5 | 30 blue print** |
| Q7 | 8 green |
| | 8 red |
| Q8 | 8 green |
| | 8 red |
| Q12 | 30 blue print** |
| Q32 | 15 black |
| Q32 reversed | 15 white |
| Q34 | 8 white |
| Q34 reversed | 8 black |
| R2 | 8 white |
| R3 | 16 blue print |
| R10 | 8 red |
| R11 | 16 blue print |
| R14 | 30 blue print |
| S1 | 14 red |
| | 1 yellow |
| T11 | 8 black |
| | 8 white |
| 1½" x 28½" strip | 8 green |
| | 8 red |
| 1½" x 16½" strip | 4 green |
| | 4 red |
| 5" x 26½" rectangle | 10 vacation print |
| 5" x 14½" rectangle | 4 vacation print |

*Refer to Steps 1–2 to cut remaining pieces.
**Reverse template for half the pieces.

## Quilt Construction:

**1.** Enlarge moonbeams pattern on page 126 onto shiny side of a 12" square of gridded freezer paper.

**2.** Refer to Gridded Freezer Paper as a Creative Tool, page 120, to code freezer paper templates, cut pieces for moonbeams, and assemble 8 blocks. Refer to photograph for color placement.

**3.** Follow block diagrams at right to make 8 Cruisin' blocks and 15 Mini-Cruisin' blocks. Join 1 Moonbeam block to top of each Cruisin' block.

**4.** Follow quilt diagram below to join red and green border strips to sides and top of Cruisin' blocks, mitering corners (see photograph). Add bases to bottom of Cruisin' blocks (pieces T11, Q7, Q8, and OP10).

**5.** Join Cruisin' blocks to make 4 vertical rows of 2 blocks each. Join 1 (5" x 14½") rectangle to top of each vertical row.

**6.** Join Mini-Cruisin' blocks to 5" x 26½" rectangles as shown in quilt diagram to make 5 vertical strips. Join vertical strips to vertical Cruisin' rows.

**7.** Follow print in border for quilting lines and outline-quilt ship and moonbeams. Quilt 1 of the 8 phases of moon in each Moonbeam block (see quilt diagram). Bind with black fabric.

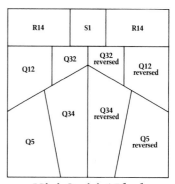

**Mini-Cruisin' Block**

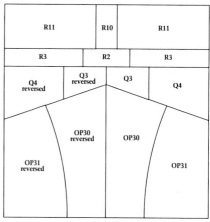

**Cruisin' Block**

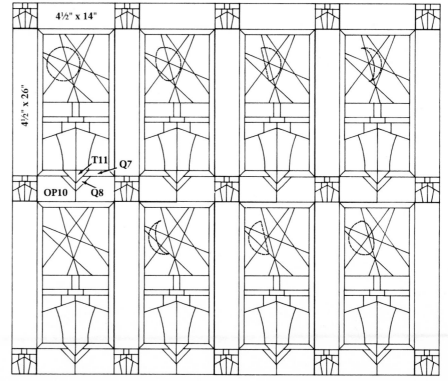

# UK Sampler

Years ago, I saw an old chintz quilt in the Victoria and Albert Museum in London. I was amazed to see the feather design appliquéd rather than used as a quilting pattern. That technique is the feature accent on this special quilted tribute to Great Britain.

My quilt begins with a center block of hexagons, whipstitched using English piecing and displaying the letters *UK* for United Kingdom. The sampler blocks have special significance. The Rails blocks represent the British rail system, linking one picturesque city to another. Quilters in England are joined by a guild, and the Guild block is taken from their logo. Finally, the British flag adorns the four outside corners.

The chintz panels were appliquéd with the feather design. I chose to mix various shades of red and blue to match the colors in the British flag.

Finished Size: 90" x 100"
Perimeter: 380"
Blocks: 4 (10"-square) Rails blocks
       4 (12"-square) Guild blocks
       4 (15" x 20") UK Flag blocks
       1 (16"-square) Center UK block

**Fabric Requirements:**

| | |
|---|---|
| Flowered chintz | 6½ yards |
| Assorted shades of blue | 2 yards |
| Assorted shades of red | 2 yards |
| Backing | 9 yards |
| Flowered chintz for binding | ⅞ yard |

## Pieces to Cut:
### Center UK Block
| | |
|---|---|
| OP11 | 45 chintz* |
| | 23 chintz** |
| Q6 | 8 chintz* |
| T16 | 14 chintz* |
| T55 | 4 chintz* |

### Rails Blocks
| | |
|---|---|
| P12 | 8 light red |
| | 8 light blue |
| | 8 dark red |
| | 8 dark blue |
| Q13 | 32 chintz |
| R20 | 4 light red |
| | 4 light blue |
| | 4 dark red |
| | 4 dark blue |
| T14 | 32 chintz |

### Guild Blocks
| | |
|---|---|
| Q18 | 32 chintz |
| S17 | 2 blue |
| | 2 red |
| T63 | 56 blue |
| | 56 red |
| | 144 chintz |
| T65 | 16 chintz |

### UK Flag Blocks
| | |
|---|---|
| OP18 | 16 red/chintz (see Step 12) |
| R18 | 4 dark red |
| R19 | 8 dark red |
| T26 | 16 dark blue |
| T27 | 16 dark blue |
| 1½" x 11½" strip | 16 chintz |
| 1¼" x 11½" strip | 16 dark red |
| ¾" x 11½" strip | 16 chintz |
| ⅞" x 9⅛" strip | 16 chintz |
| ⅞" x 6⅞" strip | 16 chintz |

### Feather Panels
| | |
|---|---|
| OP13 (center and end feathers) | 8 blue |
| | 8 red |
| OP13 | 60 blue |
| | 60 red |
| 12½" x 36½" rectangle | 4 chintz |
| OP14 (center and end feathers) | 12 blue |
| | 4 red |
| OP14 | 40 blue |
| | 48 red |
| 10½" x 16½" rectangle | 4 chintz |

| | |
|---|---|
| OP15 (center and end feathers) | 8 blue |
| | 8 red |
| OP15 | 84 blue |
| | 84 red |
| 15½" x 60½" rectangle | 2 chintz |
| 20½" x 60½" rectangle | 2 chintz |

\*Cut from dark area of chintz.
\*\*Cut from light area of chintz.

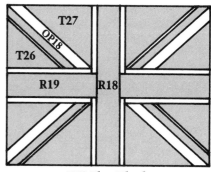

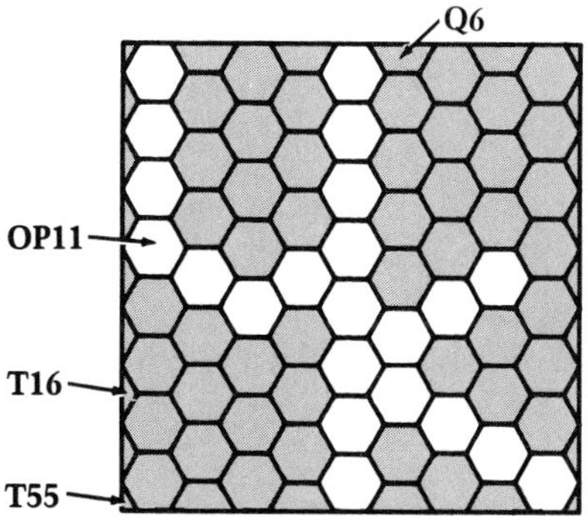

**UK Flag Block**

## Quilt Construction:
**1.** Read Quilt-and-Extend Method, page 122, before beginning.

**2.** Referring to Center UK block diagram at left, make UK block, following this quick version of the traditional English hand-piecing method. Transfer finished-size templates (without seam allowance) to dull side of gridded freezer paper as follows: OP11, 68 times; Q6, 8 times; T16, 14 times; and T55, 4 times. Cut out freezer paper templates and center and iron to wrong side of their respective fabric pieces. Finger-press seam allowances to wrong side.

**3.** With right sides facing and straight edges aligned, match and whipstitch edges to join hexagons, following Center UK block diagram for placement. Fill in edges with Q6, T55, and T16 pieces. Remove freezer paper. Finished block will measure 16½" x 16¹¹⁄₁₆".

**4.** Cut 1 (16½") square each from batting and backing. Stack backing, right side down; batting; and center block, right side up, easing the 16¹¹⁄₁₆" edges of block to fit the 16½"-square backing. Lap-quilt as desired.

**5.** Make 4 (10½" x 16½") appliquéd feather panels, using OP14 feathers, as follows: Following quilt diagram on page 60 and photograph on page 61 for placement, trace center line of feather unit on each 10½" x 16½" chintz rectangle to guide placement of appliquéd feathers.

Cut finished-size OP14 template from thin cardboard. Place template on wrong side of fabric piece. Apply

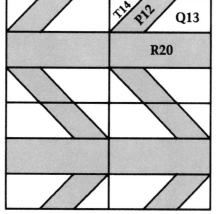

**Center UK Block**

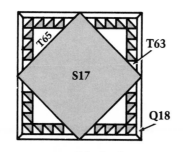

**Rails Block**

**Guild Block**

spray starch to seam allowances, fold seam allowances over edge of cardboard, and press. Remove cardboard. Place appliqués along traced line and appliqué with lightweight thread, using a running stitch. (See Appliqué Accents, page 121.) Set 2 feather panels aside.

**6.** Cut 2 backings and 2 battings to match feather panels. Add panels to Center UK block, using quilt-and-extend method.

**7.** Make 4 Rails blocks, following block diagram on page 59 and quilt photograph on page 61 for placement. Join blocks to ends of 2 remaining feather panels. Cut 2 backings and 2 battings to match units. Layer units with batting and backing. Join these 2 units to sides of center unit as shown in quilt diagram. Quilt.

**8.** Follow Step 5 to appliqué OP13 feathers to 4 (12½" x 36½") chintz rectangles. Join 2 feather panels to top and bottom edges of center unit as shown in quilt diagram. Lap-quilt as desired.

**9.** Following block diagram on page 59 and quilt photograph on page 61 for placement, make 4 Guild blocks. Join Guild blocks to ends of remaining (12½" x 36½") feather panels.

**10.** Follow Step 5 to appliqué OP15 feathers to 20½" x 60½" and 15½" x 60½" chintz panels. Set 20½" x 60½" feather panels aside. Join other 2 feather panels to the long edges of 2 Guild block units as shown in quilt diagram. Join panels to center section and quilt.

**11.** To make template for quilting pattern on Guild block, fold an 8½"

square of gridded freezer paper in half diagonally. Fold diagonally again and then again, to divide paper into 8 sections.

Transfer the UK quilting pattern on page 127 to folded freezer paper. Cut out design along traced lines through all layers. Unfold, iron to the center of Guild block, and trace around design.

**12.** To make UK Flag blocks, join 1 (1½" x 11½") chintz strip, 1 (1¼" x 11½") red strip, and 1 (¾" x 11½") chintz strip as shown in the photo-graph to make a striped band. Repeat for 3 more bands. Cut 8 OP18 pieces from striped band; reverse template and cut 8 more. Following UK Flag block diagram on page 59 for place-ment, join 1 T26 and 1 T27 to each OP18 unit.

Following UK Flag block diagram, join 1 (⅞" x 9⅛") strip to 1 long edge of each pieced rectangle. Join 1 (⅞" x 6⅞") strip to 1 short edge of each pieced rectangle. Join 1 pieced rect-angle to each long edge of 1 R19 piece. Repeat with remaining R19 piece.

Join units to long edges of R18 piece to complete flag. Repeat Step 12, 3 times for 4 flag blocks.

**13.** Join UK Flag blocks to ends of remaining feather panels. Join panels to top and bottom of quilt. Quilt panels. Bind with chintz fabric.

> ### *Bright Idea!*
> *To develop a unique signature touch, try the UK quilting pat-tern technique (see Step 11) with your own initials.*

# Singapore Stars

The teaching location was Singapore; the subject was patchwork stars. Hence the name for a stunning array of star patterns, made by Penny Wortman.

Finished Size: 44½" x 44½"
Perimeter: 178"
Blocks: 4 (10"-square) star blocks
      4 (4⅝"-square) star blocks

**Fabric Requirements:**

| | |
|---|---|
| Turquoise | 3¼ yards |
| Lt. rose | ½ yard |
| Dk. rose | 1 yard |
| Blue print | ¾ yard |
| Small black print | 1⅛ yards |
| Large black print | ⅞ yard |
| Solid white | 1 yard |
| White print | ⅛ yard |
| Backing | 1⅓ yards |
| Black for binding | ¾ yard |

**Pieces to Cut:**

**Center Star and Pieced Border**

| | |
|---|---|
| P1 | 16 turquoise |
| | 25 lt. rose |
| | 44 blue print |
| | 43 small black print |
| | 35 dk. rose |
| | 25 large black print |
| T32 | 1 lt. rose |
| | 1 dk. rose |
| | 1 blue print |
| | 1 large black print |

**Star and Cross Block**

| | |
|---|---|
| OP1 | 4 dk. rose |
| Q22 | 8 small black print* |
| S4 | 4 solid white |
| S9 | 4 dk. rose |
| | 4 turquoise |
| | 1 lt. rose |
| T5 | 4 solid white |

**Rising Star Block**

| | |
|---|---|
| P13 | 4 turquoise** |
| | 4 dk. rose |
| S4 | 4 solid white |
| S12 | 4 white print |
| T5 | 4 solid white |
| T32 | 8 large black print |
| T45 | 4 white print |

**Morning Star Block**

| | |
|---|---|
| S14 | 4 solid white |
| T42 | 4 turquoise |
| | 4 dk. rose |
| | 4 large black print |
| | 4 small black print |
| T65 | 4 solid white |

**Grandma's Star Block**

| | |
|---|---|
| S8 | 1 dk. rose |
| T14 | 4 turquoise |
| T18 | 4 solid white |
| T33 | 4 solid white |
| | 4 white print |
| T62 | 4 large black print* |
| | 4 small black print* |

**Ohio Star Block**

| | |
|---|---|
| S7 | 4 solid white |
| | 1 large black print |
| T2 | 4 solid white |
| | 8 small black print |
| | 4 turquoise |
| T13 | 2 solid white |
| T33 | 1 solid white |

**Blazing Star Block**

| | |
|---|---|
| T13 | 2 solid white |
| T22 | 8 solid white* |
| T33 | 1 solid white |
| T56 | 4 small black print** |
| | 4 turquoise |
| T61 | 4 blue print* |
| | 4 dk. rose* |

**Sawtooth Star Block**

| | |
|---|---|
| S9 | 4 solid white |
| T13 | 2 solid white |
| T33 | 1 solid white |
| T44 | 8 solid white |
| | 8 small black print |
| | 4 dk. rose |
| | 4 blue print |

**Another Star Block**

| | |
|---|---|
| S6 | 1 turquoise |
| S7 | 4 solid white |
| T2 | 4 solid white |
| | 8 small black print |
| | 4 dk. rose |
| T13 | 2 solid white |
| T33 | 1 solid white |
| T43 | 4 dk. rose |

**Solid Borders**

| | |
|---|---|
| 2¼" x 39½" strip | 4 turquoise |
| 2¼" x 46½" strip | 4 turquoise |

*Reverse template for half the pieces.
**Reverse template.

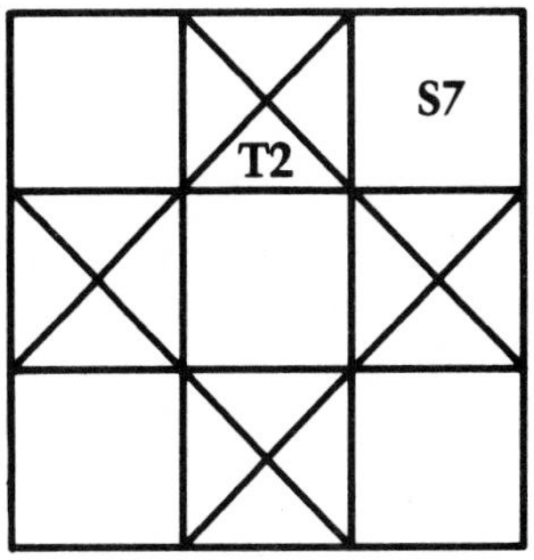

**Ohio Star Block**

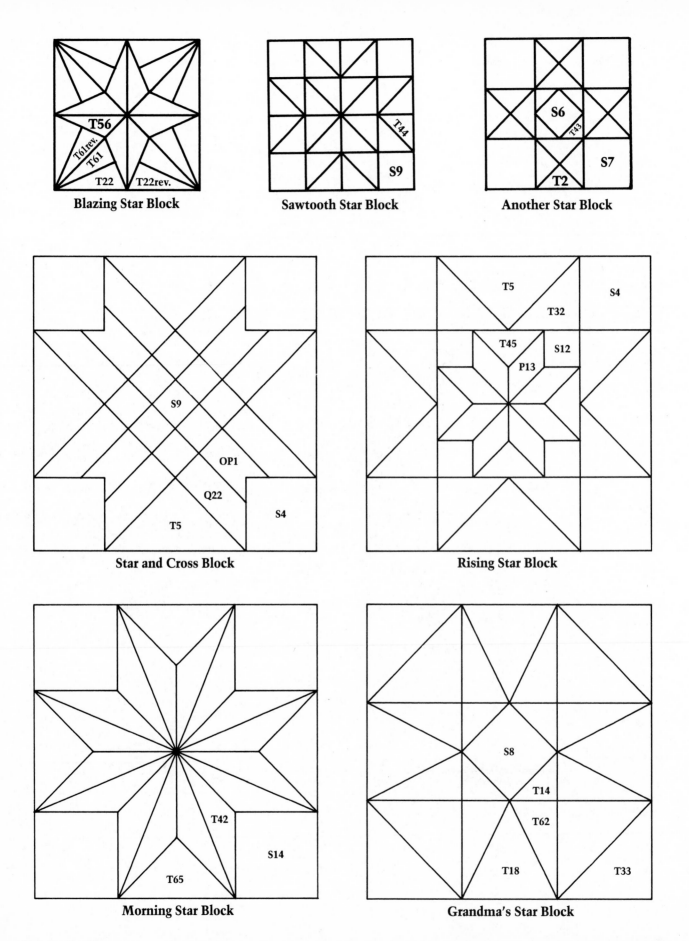

**Blazing Star Block**

**Sawtooth Star Block**

**Another Star Block**

**Star and Cross Block**

**Rising Star Block**

**Morning Star Block**

**Grandma's Star Block**

## Quilt Construction:

**1.** Follow block diagrams and quilt photograph on pages 62–64 to make the 8 star blocks. Complete small blocks by joining T13 and T33 triangles as shown in quilt diagram. Set aside.

**2.** Follow quilt diagram at right and quilt photograph to make center star.

**3.** Follow quilt diagram to join star blocks to center star.

**4.** Follow quilt diagram and quilt photograph to make inner border and to join all borders to quilt, mitering corners.

**5.** Quilt as desired. Bind with black fabric.

### Bright Idea!
*The key to success in piecing all acute-angle patterns, such as diamonds or hard-to-sew inside right angles, is to stop at the corner dot and lock the seam in place by backstitching, allowing for a free-floating seam. Lift needle, break off thread, and insert needle at corner dot on other side of seam allowance.*

# Amish Images

Drive slowly into the world of the Amish and experience their gentle ways and peaceful existence. The bright red and gold patches that form the hazard signs on the backs of their somber buggies provide lasting images—and great quilt inspiration!

Finished Size: 77½" x 102"
Perimeter: 359"
Blocks: 18 (11" x 16") Horse and Buggy
    blocks
    2 (11" x 13½") appliquéd word
    blocks
    60 hazard sign triangles

**Fabric Requirements:**

| | |
|---|---|
| Assorted red and gold | 5 yards total |
| Black print | 4 yards |
| Gold print | 3⅞ yards |
| Backing | 6 yards |
| Black print for binding | ⅞ yard |

**Pieces to Cut:**

| | |
|---|---|
| OP4* | 18 gold print |
| OP5 | 18 black print |
| OP16* | 18 black print** |
| P3* | 18 gold print |
| P4* | 18 black print** |
| P11* | 18 black print** |
| Q19 | 180 assorted red and gold |
| T24 | 50 black print |
| T25 | 60 assorted red and gold |
| T28* | 18 gold print |
| T29* | 18 gold print |
| T40 | 18 assorted red and gold |
| | 50 black print |
| T47* | 20 black print |
| T50* | 20 black print |
| 1½" x 16½" strip | 18 gold print |
| 3" x 9" rectangle | 18 gold print |
| 8" x 10½" rectangle | 18 gold print |
| 11½" x 14" rectangle | 2 gold print |
| "Amish" appliqué | 1 black print |
| "Images" appliqué | 1 black print |

*Reverse template for half the pieces.
**Cut pieces from reverse side of fabric.

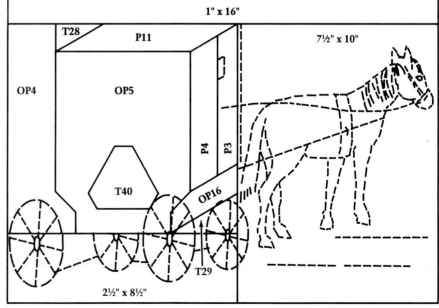

**Quilt Construction:**

**1.** Referring to quilt diagram, assemble 10 horizontal rows of hazard signs as follows: Join narrow borders (Q19) to large triangles (T25) to form 60 hazard signs. Join T24 triangles to left edges of 50 hazard signs as shown. Join black T40 triangles to right edges of signs as shown. Join these units in 10 horizontal rows of 5 each. Join 1 remaining hazard sign to left edge of each horizontal row. Join 1 black T47 to right edge and 1 reversed T47 to left edge of each horizontal row (see quilt diagram). Join 1 black T50 to right edge and 1 reversed T50 to left edge of each horizontal row (see quilt diagram). Join horizontal rows as shown in quilt diagram, balancing red and gold colors.

**2.** Enlarge "Amish" and "Images" word appliqués on page 124. Enlarge Horse and Buggy pattern on page 125.

**3.** Following block diagram on page 67, piece 18 Horse and Buggy blocks. (*Note:* 9 buggies face in 1 direction, 9 in the other.) Clip corners from the 18 red and gold T40 triangles. Appliqué to backs of buggies. Transfer quilting lines for horse and wheels to right sides of blocks with black indelible pen.

**4.** Referring to quilt diagram on page 69 for placement, appliqué words to 11½" x 14" rectangles. Set aside.

**5.** To make borders, join Horse and Buggy blocks and appliquéd word blocks as shown in quilt diagram. Join borders to quilt top.

**6.** Outline-quilt along lines drawn on Horse and Buggy blocks (see detail photograph above). Outline-quilt around all buggy pieces. Quilt around words in the appliquéd word blocks. Quilt a large A (for Amish) inside each hazard sign T25 triangle. Quilt a triangle inside each black T24 triangle.

**7.** Bind with black print fabric.

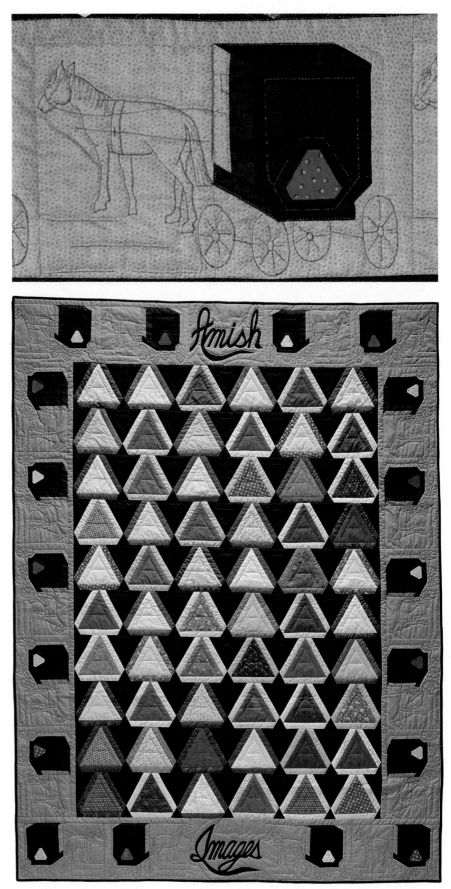

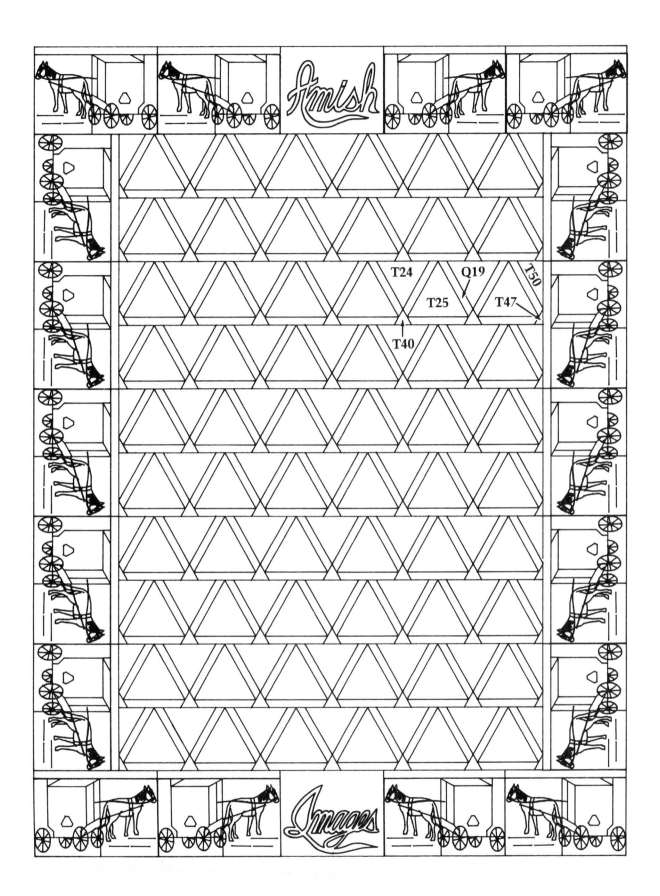

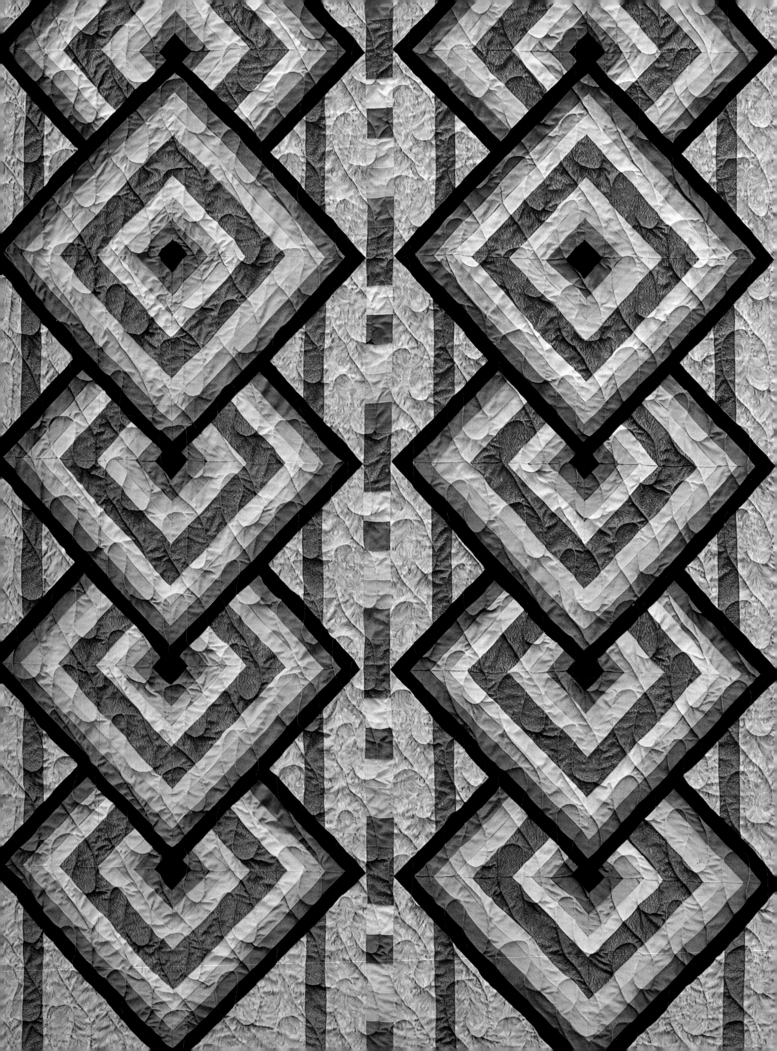

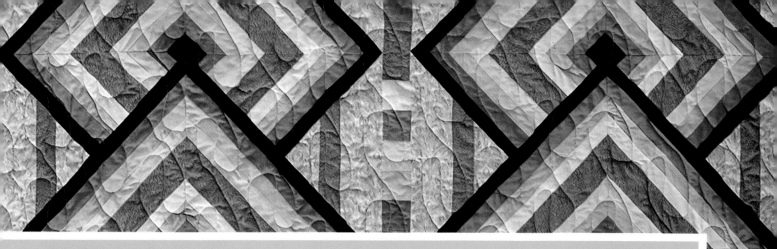

# STRING FEVER

Regular bands, exact measurements, and a rotary cutter help update these variations of the old-time string quilt.

*Hipp Strip*

# Hipp Strip

Graduated shades of coral and aqua give this quilt a southwestern look.

Finished Size: 113" x 119"
Perimeter: 464"
Blocks: 64 (14⅛"-square) blocks

## Fabric Requirements:

| | |
|---|---|
| Paisley print | 3⅜ yards |
| Purple print | 2⅛ yards |
| Black | 3 yards |
| Dk. aqua | 1⅛ yards |
| Med. aqua | 1⅛ yards |
| Lt. aqua | 1⅛ yards |
| Dk. coral | 1⅛ yards |
| Med. coral | 1⅛ yards |
| Lt. coral | 1⅛ yards |
| Backing | 10 yards |
| Paisley print for binding | 1 yard |

## Pieces to Cut:

| | | |
|---|---|---|
| A* | 32 | pieced coral-to-aqua stripe |
| | 32 | pieced aqua-to-coral stripe |
| B* | 24 | pieced coral-to-aqua stripe |
| | 24 | pieced aqua-to-coral stripe |
| Q37 | 48 | purple print |
| Q38 | 48 | paisley print |
| Q39 | 16 | paisley print |
| Q40 | 16 | purple print |
| T69 | 48 | paisley print |
| T70 | 16 | paisley print |

*See Steps 1–4.

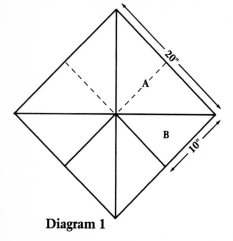

**Diagram 1**

20"

A

B

10"

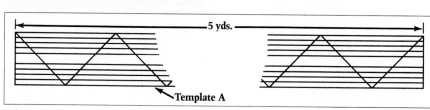

5 yds.

Template A

**Diagram 2**

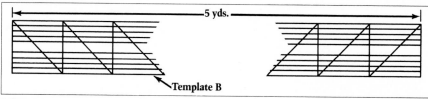

5 yds.

Template B

**Diagram 3**

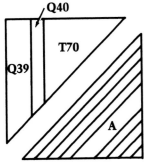

**Diagram 4**

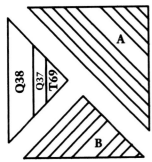

**Diagram 5**

## Quilt Construction:

**1.** Make templates A and B by folding a 20" square of paper as shown in Diagram 1. Open square. Cut out templates A and B. Redraw templates, adding ¼" seam allowance all around.

**2.** Cut and piece 3 shades of coral, 3 shades of aqua, and black fabrics into 1½"-x-5-yard bias strips. Cut and piece purple print fabric into 2½"-x-5-yard bias strips.

**3.** Join long edges of bias strips in order shown in photograph (black, dk. coral, med. coral, lt. coral, purple print, lt. aqua, med. aqua, dk. aqua, black) to make a 9-color striped band. Repeat to make 5 more bands.

**4.** Place base of template A on black and cut 32 striped triangles, shading from coral at outside to aqua at center point, and 32 shading from aqua at outside to coral at center point. (See Diagram 2 for triangle placement.) Place base of template B on black and cut 24 triangles, shading from coral at outside to aqua at center point, and 24 shading from aqua at outside to coral at center point. (See Diagram 3 for triangle placement.)

**5.** Follow Diagram 4 to make 16 blocks. Follow Diagram 5 to make 48 blocks..

**6.** Join pieced blocks as shown in quilt diagram to make an 8-block-by-2-block vertical row. Repeat to make 3 more rows.

**7.** Cut 2 (2½" x 45") strips each on straight grain from lt. aqua, dk. aqua, lt. coral, med. coral, and dk. coral. Cut 4 (2½" x 45") strips from purple print. Join long edges of purple print, lt. aqua, dk. aqua, lt. coral, med. coral, dk. coral, and purple print strips to make 2 (7-color) bands. Cut across bands to make 24 (2½"-wide) multicolor strips. Join 8 strips to make 1 sashing strip. Repeat twice. Join rows with sashing strips.

**8.** Quilt as desired. Bind with paisley print fabric.

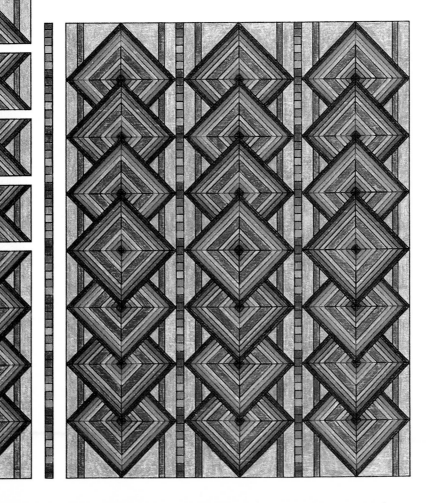

# Woven Wonder

Here is another banded beauty, this one stitched by Judy Rankin. For an easy solution to piecing this awesome block, which I designed with inspiration from a graphic puzzle, follow the step-by-step diagrams. Six coordinated aqua fabrics weave in and out of mitered pastel frames.

Finished Size: 82" x 102"
Perimeter: 368"
Blocks: 10 (18" x 20") A blocks
10 (20" x 22") B blocks

## Fabric Requirements:

| | |
|---|---|
| Dk. rose print | 1¾ yards |
| Rose print #1 | 2 yards |
| Rose print #2 | 1⅝ yards |
| Rose print #3 | 1⅝ yards |
| Rose print #4 | 1⅝ yards |
| Dk. aqua | ⅞ yard |
| Lt. aqua | ⅞ yard |
| Aqua print #1 | ⅞ yard |
| Aqua print #2 | ⅞ yard |
| Aqua print #3 | ⅞ yard |
| Aqua print #4 | ⅞ yard |
| Backing | 6 yards |
| Aqua print for binding | ⅞ yard |

## Pieces to Cut:

| | |
|---|---|
| Q35 | 80 pieced rose stripe* |
| R7 | 98 dk. rose print |
| S3 | 80 dk. rose print |
| | 30 rose print #1 |
| Trapezoid | 40 pieced rose stripe* |
| 6½" x 10½" rectangle | |
| | 20 pieced aqua stripe* |
| 6½" x 8½" rectangle | |
| | 30 pieced aqua stripe* |
| 2½" x 6½" rectangle | |
| | 17 pieced aqua stripe* |
| 6½" square | 8 pieced aqua stripe* |

*See Steps 1–4. Reverse template for half the pieces.

## Quilt Construction:

**1.** To make trapezoid template, extend template Q35 from corner dots 3" and place on fold (see template).
**2.** Cut all print fabric into 1½"-wide strips lengthwise or crosswise.
**3.** Join 1½"-wide strips of rose prints #1–4 in order shown in photograph to make 4½"-wide bands. Cut Q35 and trapezoid pieces from these bands.
**4.** Join 1½"-wide strips of 6 aqua prints and solids in order shown in photograph to make 6½"-wide bands. Cut 6½" x 10½", 6½" x 8½", 2½" x 6½", and 6½"-square pieces from these bands.
**5.** Make 10 A blocks and 10 B blocks, following Diagrams 1 and 2. Make 5 strips from R7 and S3 pieces and 2½" x 6½" pieced strips, following Diagram 3 on page 76.
**6.** To make Row 1, join 2 A blocks, 2 B blocks, and 1 pieced strip as shown in Diagram 3. Repeat process to make Rows 3 and 5. To make bottom border, piece strip as shown and join to bottom of Row 5 (see Diagram 4 on page 76).
**7.** Join blocks and strips as shown in Diagram 3 to make Rows 2 and 4.
**8.** Lap-quilt rows as desired.
**9.** Follow Diagram 4 to join rows (see Block-to-Block Connections, page 121). Bind with aqua print.

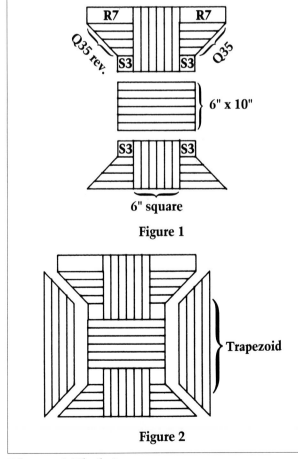

**Figure 1**

**Figure 2**

**Diagram 1: Block A**

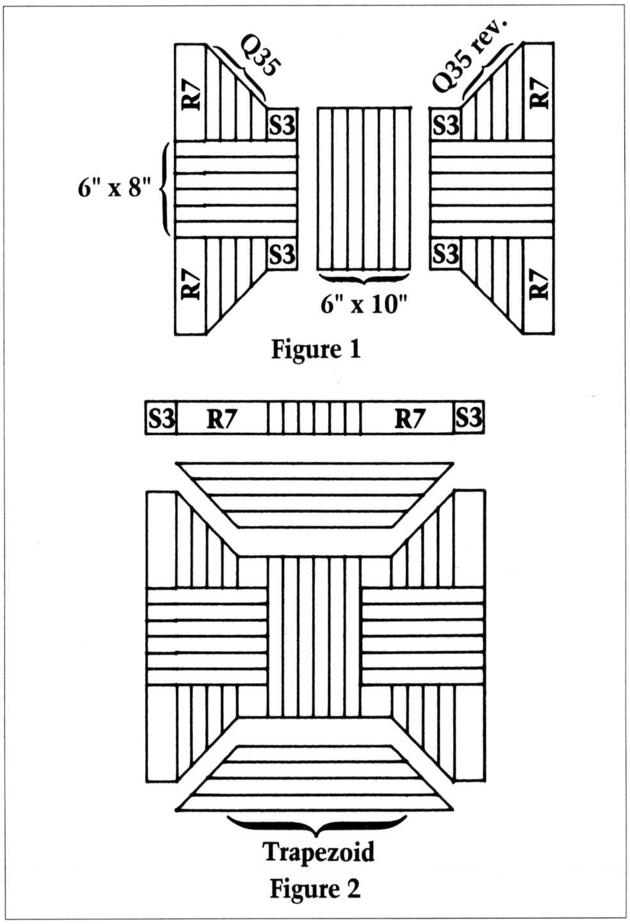

**Diagram 2: Block B**

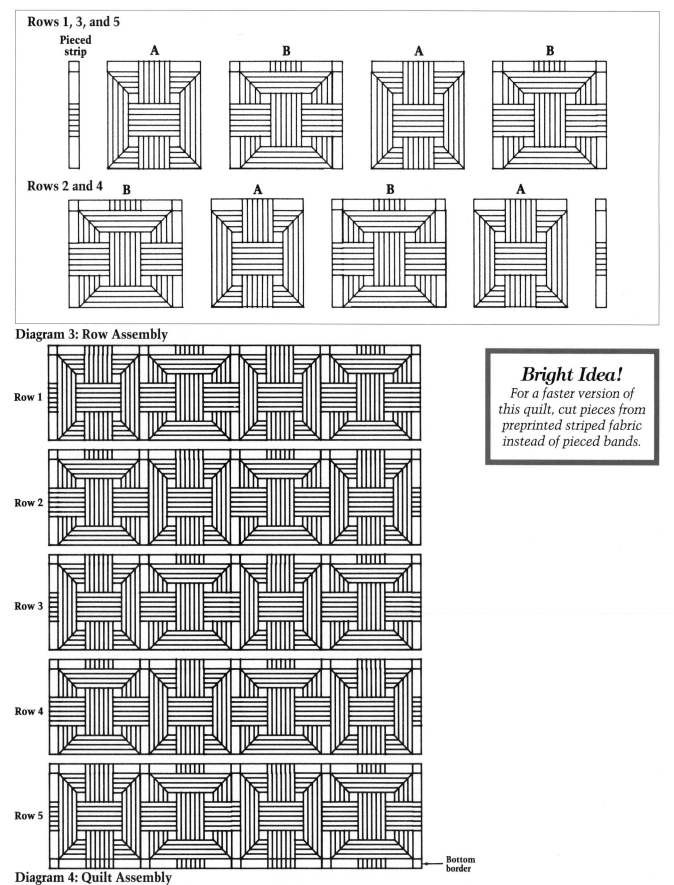

**Rows 1, 3, and 5**

Pieced strip

A      B      A      B

**Rows 2 and 4**

B      A      B      A

**Diagram 3: Row Assembly**

Row 1

Row 2

Row 3

Row 4

Row 5

Bottom border

**Diagram 4: Quilt Assembly**

### Bright Idea!

*For a faster version of this quilt, cut pieces from preprinted striped fabric instead of pieced bands.*

# Strawberries and Strings Vest

Using a variation of the *Woven Wonder* block, create a zippered vest. These instructions are for a medium size. Increase or decrease at the side edges of the block for larger or smaller sizes.

## Material Requirements:

| | |
|---|---|
| Dk. green print | ¼ yard |
| Red print | ¼ yard |
| Yellow print | ¼ yard |
| White | ¼ yard |
| Strawberry print | ¼ yard |
| Black print | ⅛ yard |
| Large gray print | ⅛ yard |
| 3 small gray prints | ⅛ yard each |
| Lining | ¾ yard |
| Strawberry print for binding | ⅜ yard |
| 1"-wide elastic | 1 yard |
| ⅛"-wide satin ribbon | 12" red |
| | 12" yellow |
| | 12" green |

20" separating zipper

## Pieces to Cut:

| | |
|---|---|
| Q35 | 8 pieced stripe |
| R7 | 16 strawberry print |
| S3 | 16 strawberry print |
| Trapezoid | 4 pieced stripe |
| 6½" x 10½" rectangle | 2 black/gray stripe |
| 6½" x 8½" rectangle | 4 black/gray stripe |
| 2½" x 6½" rectangle | 4 black/gray stripe |
| 2½" x 3" rectangle | 2 strawberry print |

## Vest Construction:

**1.** Follow Steps 1–4 for *Woven Wonder* quilt, page 75, substituting fabrics in Material Requirements for rose and aqua fabrics.

**2.** Following diagram below, make 1 block (shaded area) for back and 2 half-blocks (unshaded areas) for front. (*Note:* Add ¼" seam allowance to half trapezoids when cutting.)

**3.** Join vest front and back sections at side seams (see diagram). Trim blocks to make neck edge and armholes as shown in diagram.

**4.** Separate zipper. With teeth pointing away from edge of vest, place bottom of zipper 2¼" from bottom of vest and stitch zipper to center front.

**5.** With right sides facing, lay vest on top of lining fabric, aligning front edges of vest with grain of lining fabric. Sew lining to vest along bottom and front, stopping 2" from bottom. Trim lining fabric even with vest. Turn and press. Topstitch across bottom of vest.

**6.** For button tab at waist, trim 1 end of each 2½" x 3" rectangle to a point. With right sides facing, sew tab along sides and point, leaving opening on straight end. Turn and press. Work buttonhole near pointed end (see photograph).

**7.** Make casing along bottom of vest by stitching in-the-ditch along first horizontal seam line in blocks at bottom of vest (see diagram).

**8.** Stitch raw edge of tab to 1 end of elastic. Attach safety pin to other end of elastic. Thread elastic through casing, safety pin first. Remove safety pin and stitch free end of elastic in place through seam allowances at front edge of vest. Stitch tab in place through seam allowances at opposite edge of vest. Sew button in place.

**9.** With right sides facing, join vest front to back at shoulder seams, leaving lining shoulder seams free. Turn under seam allowances on lining shoulder seams and slipstitch together. Bind neck edge and armholes with strawberry print fabric.

**10.** Using strawberry cutouts from print fabric, make 3 stuffed strawberries. Tie bow in 1 end of 1 length of ribbon. Tack bow to top of strawberry. Repeat with remaining ribbon for other 2 strawberries. Tie free ends of ribbons to zipper tab.

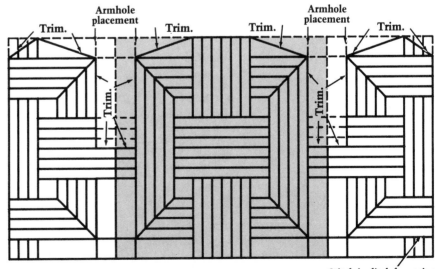

**Vest Construction**

# Interlock

This intriguing design is a visual tongue twister. But its construction is simpler than it might seem. The entire quilt is made from just nine repetitions of one block. Add a series of two-inch borders for an intricate-looking puzzle that is sure to be a conversation starter.

Finished Size: 89½" x 97½"
Perimeter: 374"
Blocks: 9 (28½"-square) Interlock blocks

**Fabric Requirements:**

| | |
|---|---|
| Print | 6½ yards |
| White | 6½ yards |
| Backing | 8⅝ yards |
| Fabric for binding | 1 yard |

**Pieces to Cut:**

| | | |
|---|---|---|
| 25" square | | 9 print |
| 2½" x 31" strip | | 36 white |
| 2½" x 26" strip | | 18 white |
| 2½" x 36" strip | | 18 white |
| 2½" x 6½" strip | | 4 white |
| 2½" x 29" strip | | 18 white |
| | | 6 print |

**Quilt Construction:**
1. Following Diagram 1, fold 1 (25") print square diagonally; press fold to crease. With square still folded, measure 2¾" from fold and mark. Measure 2½" from first marked line

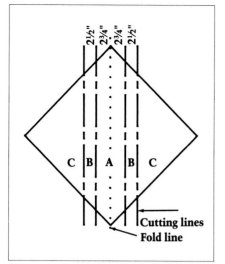

**Diagram 1**

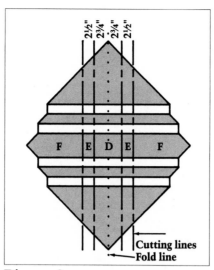

**Diagram 3**

and mark again. Cut along marked lines to make 5 sections as shown in Diagram 1.

**2.** With bias fabric against feed dogs, join a 2½" x 31" white strip to each side of section A (see Diagram 2, Figure 1).

**3.** Join a section B to each 2½" x 31" strip (see Diagram 2, Figure 2).

**4.** Join a 2½" x 26" white strip to each section B (see Diagram 2, Figure 3).

**5.** Join a triangle C to each 2½" x 26" strip (see Diagram 2, Figure 4).

**6.** Following Diagram 3, refer to Step 1 above to cut pieced unit into 5 sections.

**7.** Join a 2½" x 36" white strip to each side of section D (see Diagram 4, Figure 1).

**8.** Join a section E to each 2½" x 36" strip (see Diagram 4, Figure 2).

**9.** Join a 2½" x 31" white strip to each section E (see Diagram 4, Figure 3).

**10.** Join a section F to each 2½" x 31" strip (see Diagram 4, Figure 4).

**11.** Trim pieced unit as shown in Diagram 4, Figure 4, to form a 29" square. (See Diagram 5 for finished block.)

**12.** Repeat Steps 1–11, to make 8 more blocks.

**13.** Following quilt diagram, join blocks. Join 2½" x 29" strips and 2½" x 6½" strips to make borders. Join borders to quilt top.

**14.** Quilt as desired. Bind.

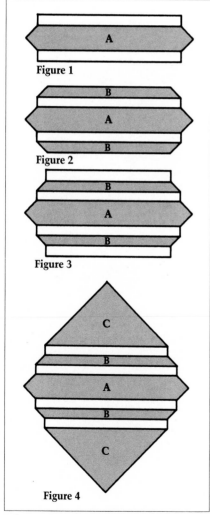

**Diagram 2**

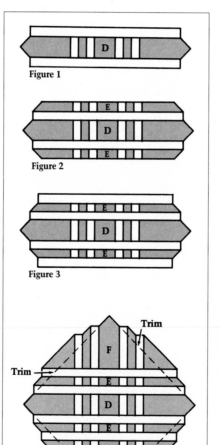

**Diagram 4**

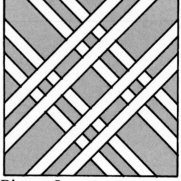

**Diagram 5**

# Manteca Ribbons

When the Manteca Quilters of Northern California asked me to design their raffle quilt, I went to work with enthusiasm. I used peach and navy fabrics to create striped bands that seem to overlap around the quilt's center square. Note how I used the reverse sides of the fabrics to provide subtle shading.

Finished Size: 108" x 108"
Perimeter: 432"

**Fabric Requirements:**

| | |
|---|---|
| Navy | 2½ yards |
| Navy print #1 | 1¾ yards |
| Navy print #2 | 1¾ yards |
| Navy print #3 | 1¾ yards |
| Navy print #4 | 2¾ yards |
| Peach | 2 yards |
| Dk. peach print | 2 yards |
| Lt. peach print | 2 yards |
| Backing | 9¼ yards |
| Navy for binding | 1 yard |

**Pieces to Cut:**

| | |
|---|---|
| T37 | 36 striped band |
| | 16 lt. peach print |
| | 16 navy |
| | 8 dk. peach print |
| | 8 peach |
| | 8 navy print #1 |
| | 8 navy print #2 |
| T37A | 8 navy |
| | 4 lt. peach print |
| 12½" square | 4 lt. peach print |
| 17½" square | 1 navy |
| | 4 navy print #4 |
| 2½" x 61" strip | 4 navy print #1 |
| (Group 1) | 4 navy print #2 |
| | 4 navy print #3 |
| | 4 navy print #4 |
| | 4 dk. peach print |
| | 4 peach |
| 2½" x 25½" strip | 12 navy print #1* |
| (Group 2) | 12 navy print #2* |
| | 12 navy print #3* |
| | 12 navy print #4* |
| | 12 dk. peach print* |
| | 12 peach |

| | |
|---|---|
| 2½" x 65" strip | 8 navy print #1 |
| (Group 3) | 8 navy print #4 |
| | 8 dk. peach print |
| | 8 peach |

*Cut from reverse side of fabric.

**Quilt Construction:**

**1.** Following photograph for color placement, join Group 1 fabric strips to form 4 (6-stripe) bands. Join Group 2 fabric strips to form 12 (6-stripe) bands. Join Group 3 fabric strips to form 8 (4-stripe) bands. Following Diagram 1 for measurements, cut 4 pieces from Group 1 bands, adding ¼" seam allowance. Following Diagram 2 for measurements, cut 4 pieces from Group 1 bands and 8 pieces from Group 2 bands, adding ¼" seam allowance. (Reverse template for half of these.) From Group 3 bands, cut 36 T37 pieces for border.

**2.** Following quilt diagram and photograph for placement, join all pieces to make quilt top. Quilt as desired. Bind with navy fabric.

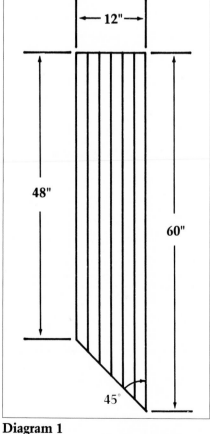

**Diagram 1**

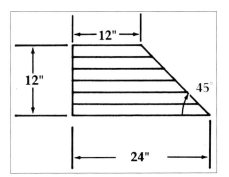

**Diagram 2**

## *Piecing Suggestion*

To complete piecing quilt top, join 1 rectangular unit to top of square, leaving final ½" of seam unstitched. Proceed counter-clockwise to join remaining 3 rectangular units to center square. Join borders, mitering corners.

# Baby Buggy Boomers

Many years ago, I received a small stack of string-pieced blocks, not enough to complete a quilt. They were from outdated fabrics, but I matched them with my current fabric supply to string-piece enough blocks, using pages from mail-order catalogs as foundations, for this baby quilt.

The buggy has a pocket for carrying an extra diaper, baby's favorite toy, or some other traveling necessity.

Finished Size: 68" x 74"
Perimeter: 284"
Blocks: 50 (7" x 10") string-pieced
blocks
3 (11"-square) string-pieced
buggy blocks
1 (11"-square) appliquéd
buggy handle block
2 (11½" x 13½") appliquéd
wheel blocks

**Fabric Requirements:**

| | |
|---|---|
| Scraps for strings | 4½ yards total |
| Pink print | 1⅛ yards |
| Pink stripe | 2 yards |
| White rickrack | ¾ yard |
| Narrow white piping | 1½ yards |
| Black bias tape (½" wide) | |
| | 5 yards |
| Backing | 6¾ yards |
| Pink stripe for binding | |
| | ¾ yard |

**Pieces to Cut:**

| | |
|---|---|
| 11½" square | 3 pink print |
| 11½" x 13½" rectangle | |
| | 2 pink print |
| 1½" x 14½" strip | 2 pink stripe |
| 1½" x 21½" strip | 2 pink stripe |
| 1½" x 70½" strip | 2 pink stripe |
| 2½" x 23½" strip | 4 pink stripe |
| 2½" x 22½" strip | 2 pink stripe |
| 2½" x 70½" strip | 2 pink stripe |

**Quilt Construction:**

1. To make string-pieced blocks, you will need 53 sheets of paper for stabilizers. (Pages from old catalogs work well.)

2. String-piece 25 blocks diagonally across rectangle, with strips running from upper left corner to lower right corner. (See Sew and Flip Method, page 122.) String-piece 25 more blocks

in same manner, with strips running from upper right corner to lower left corner. Trim blocks to 7½" x 10½". Remove paper foundations.

**3.** To make templates for piecing buggy sections, use a compass to draw a quarter-circle arc on an 11" square of paper. Cut the 2 sections apart. Trace sections 3 times, adding ¼" seam allowance. Cut out templates. String-piece scraps onto quarter-circle templates. Using remaining templates, cut 3 pieces from pink print. Join 1 quarter-circle to each pink print piece to form 3 blocks, sandwiching in rickrack on 1 block and piping on 2 blocks (see photograph). Remove paper foundations.

**4.** To make pocket, use 1 string-pieced quarter-circle block with piping trim. To face pocket, with right sides facing, pin 1 (11½") pink print square to a string-pieced quarter-circle block with piping. Sew across side of block that will border appliquéd buggy handle block above it (see diagram). Turn and press. With right side of another 11½" pink print square facing wrong side of faced block, baste the 3 squares together along the 3 raw edges.

**5.** Cut a 12" piece of black bias tape and appliqué to remaining 11½" pink print square to form handle (see diagram for placement).

**6.** Set the 4 buggy blocks together (see photograph and quilt diagram for placement). Two blocks with piping should be on bottom; handle block and block with rickrack should be on top.

**7.** To make buggy wheel blocks, use remaining black bias tape to appliqué free-form wheels to 11½" x 13½" rectangles (see photograph). Join buggy wheel blocks to bottom of buggy.

**8.** Join 4 string-pieced blocks, 2 across and 2 down, having all diagonals radiating from center of 4-block unit (see diagram). Join 1 (1½" x 14½") strip to each side of unit. Join 1 (2½" x 22½") strip to top of unit. Join this unit to top of baby buggy unit.

**9.** Join 6 string-pieced blocks, 2 across and 3 down. Join 1 (1½" x 21½") strip to each side of unit. Join 1 (2½" x 22½") strip to bottom of unit. Join unit to bottom of buggy unit as shown in diagram.

**10.** Refer to quilt diagram to make 2 panels of string-pieced blocks, 2 across and 10 down. Attach 1 (1½" x 70½") strip to inside of each unit. Attach 1 (2½" x 70½") strip to outside of each unit. Attach 1 (2½" x 23½") strip to top and bottom of each unit (see diagram).

**11.** Machine-quilt vertical panels with narrow zigzag stitching as desired. See Backing Accents, page 122, to join panels. Bind quilt with pink stripe fabric.

# Log Lanterns

The Log Cabin quilt, an American favorite and a must for every quilt collection, is classic in style and often novel in color arrangement. The *Log Lanterns* quilt is made from two block designs. Blocks are set together with like colors adjoining to form "lanterns."

Karen Pervier is the proud maker of this quilt. Wendy Crigger did the quilting.

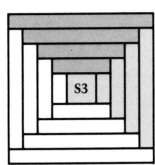

**Block A**

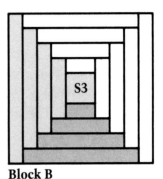

**Block B**

| Fabric key | |
|---|---|
| ▨ | Red |
| ▢ | Green |
| ☐ | White |

Finished Size: 60" x 90"
Perimeter: 300"
Blocks:  20 (10"-square) A blocks
20 (10"-square) B blocks

### Fabric Requirements:

| | |
|---|---|
| Red | 2 yards |
| Green | 2 yards |
| White | 4 yards |
| Border print | 2¾ yards |
| Backing | 6 yards |
| Green for binding | ⅞ yard |

### Pieces to Cut:

| | |
|---|---|
| S3 | 40 green |
| 5½" x 50½" border strip | 2 border print |
| 5½" x 90½" border strip | 2 border print |

### Quilt Construction:

**1.** Cut each color in continuous 1½"-wide strips down length of fabric. Following quilt block diagrams, make 20 A blocks and 20 B blocks. As you join each color to center square (S3), trim strip to desired length, building around center square.

**2.** Following quilt diagram for color placement, set blocks together in 5 rows of 8 blocks each. Join rows.

**3.** Join 5½" x 50½" border strips to top and bottom of quilt. Join 5½" x 90½" border strips to sides of quilt.

**4.** Quilt as desired. Bind with green fabric.

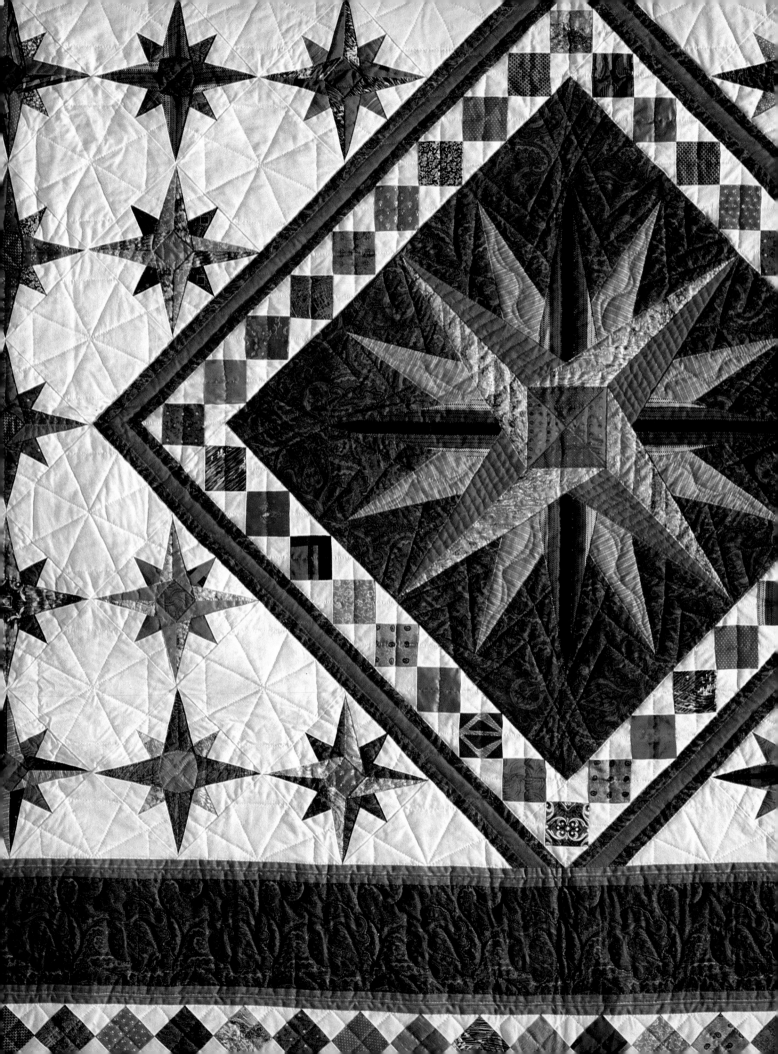

# WARM THE WALLS

Quilts take on star status when they appear on the walls of banks, corporate offices, car dealerships, and even hospitals.

*Golden Threads, Silver Needles II*

# Golden Threads, Silver Needles I

When the president of a bank in my hometown of Hendersonville, North Carolina, asked me to design a quilt to decorate the bank's new building, I was excited. By working closely with the architect and decorators, I was able to create a quilt that complemented the completed building's decor.

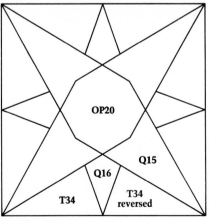

**Caribe Star**

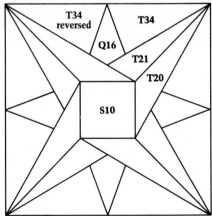

**Split Star**

Finished Size: 63" x 132"
Perimeter: 390"
Blocks: 28 (6"-square) Caribe Star blocks
24 (6"-square) Split Star blocks
1 (24"-square) Center Split Star block

## Fabric Requirements:

| | |
|---|---|
| White | 3½ yards |
| Paisley | 3¾ yards |
| Gold | ⅜ yard |
| Rust | 3⅝ yards |
| Assorted prints and solids | 3⅝ yards total |
| Backing | 8 yards |
| Paisley for binding | 1 yard |

## Quilt Construction:

**1.** Follow block diagrams to make 1 Center Split Star block, 28 Caribe Star blocks, and 24 Split Star blocks. Make and join borders to Center Split Star block, as shown in quilt diagram.

**2.** Cut each 6⅞" square in half diagonally to make 32 side triangles. Cut 7¼" square into quarters diagonally to make corner triangles.

**3.** Follow quilt diagram to set center block, star blocks, and solid squares and triangles together.

**4.** Follow quilt diagram to add 3 inner borders by joining 1¼" strips and 6¼" strips to quilt, mitering corners.

**5.** Piece outer border and join to quilt.

**6.** Quilt as desired. Bind with paisley fabric.

### Pieces to Cut:

| | | | |
|---|---|---|---|
| OP20 | 28 assorted | T34 | 416 white* |
| OP32 | 4 paisley | T59/T60** | 4 rust |
| OP33 | 16 paisley | 6½" square | 36 white*** |
| Q15 | 112 assorted | 6⅞" square | 16 white*** |
| Q16 | 208 assorted | 7¼" square | 1 white*** |
| Q30 | 8 gold | ⅞" x 32¼" strip | 4 paisley |
| Q31 | 4 assorted | 1¼" x 115½" strip | 2 rust |
| S5 | 1 assorted | 1¼" x 46½" strip | 2 rust |
| S10 | 24 assorted | 1¼" x 128½" strip | 2 rust |
| S13 | 162 assorted | 1¼" x 59½" strip | 2 rust |
| T3 | 32 white | 6¼" x 58" strip | 2 paisley |
| T4 | 308 white | 6¼" x 127" strip | 2 paisley |
| T20 | 96 assorted | | |
| T21 | 96 assorted | | |

*Reverse template for half the pieces.
**Join T59 and T60 to make 1 template.
***Cut edge of square on bias.

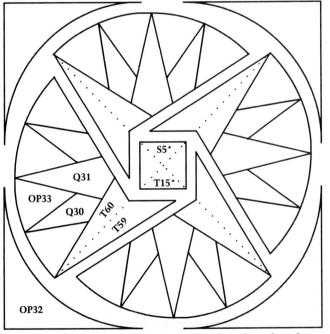

**Center Split Star**  (*Use 1 S5 for *Golden Threads, Silver Needles I*; Use 4 T15 triangles for *Golden Threads, Silver Needles II*.)

After I made *Golden Threads, Silver Needles I* for the bank in Hendersonville, I wanted a quilt like it for myself. So I made another one—but with a few changes.

Finished Size: 63" x 102"
Perimeter: 330"
Blocks: 14 (6") Caribe Star blocks
18 (6") Split Star blocks
1 (24") Center Split Star block

## Fabric Requirements:
| | |
|---|---|
| White | 2⅞ yards |
| Paisley | 3½ yards |
| Dk. red | 1 yard |
| Red marbleized | ⅜ yard |
| Lt. red | ⅛ yard |
| Red/blue/black stripe | ⅛ yard |
| Aqua | ¼ yard |
| Assorted prints and solids | 2 yards total |
| Red/blue stripe | 2¾ yards |
| Backing | 6 yards |
| Paisley for binding | ⅞ yard |

## Pieces to Cut:
| | |
|---|---|
| OP20 | 14 assorted |
| OP32 | 4 paisley |
| OP33 | 16 paisley |
| Q15 | 56 assorted |
| Q16 | 128 assorted |
| Q30 | 8 aqua |
| Q31 | 4 red/blue/black stripe |
| S10 | 18 assorted |
| S13 | 142 assorted |
| T3 | 32 white |
| T4 | 268 white |
| T15 | 2 dk. red 2 lt. red |
| T20 | 72 assorted |
| T21 | 72 assorted |
| T34 | 256 white* |
| T59 | 4 dk. red |
| T60 | 4 red marbleized |
| 6½" square | 20 white** |
| 6⅞" square | 12 white** |
| 7¼" square | 1 white** |
| 2¼" x 36½" strip | 4 paisley/red pieced stripe |
| 1¼" x 46½" strip | 2 red/blue stripe |
| 1¼" x 85½" strip | 2 red/blue stripe |
| 6¼" x 58½" strip | 2 paisley |
| 6¼" x 97" strip | 2 paisley |
| 1¼" x 59½" strip | 2 red/blue stripe |
| 1¼" x 98½" strip | 2 red/blue stripe |

*Reverse template for half the pieces.
**Cut edge of square on bias.

## Quilt Construction:
**1.** Follow block diagrams on pages 90–91 to make 14 Caribe Star blocks, 18 Split Star blocks, and 1 Center Split Star block. Note that compass in Center Split Star block has been turned ⅛ of circle. Make and join pieced borders to Center Split Star.
**2.** Cut each of the 6⅞" squares in half diagonally to make 24 side triangles. Cut 7¼" square into quarters to make 4 corner triangles.
**3.** Follow quilt diagram to set center block, star blocks, and squares and triangles together.
**4.** Join inner borders to quilt in the order that they appear in quilt diagram and photograph, mitering corners.
**5.** Make outer pieced border. Join to quilt. Quilt. Bind with paisley fabric.

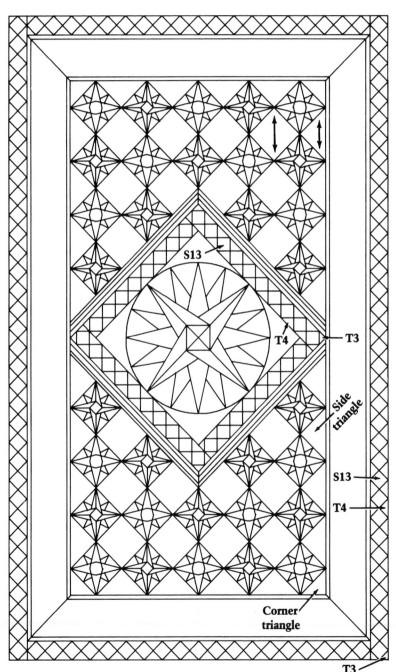

# Car Star

A new car dealership nestled in the Blue Ridge Mountains is the setting for this quilted wall hanging. In this piece, the traditional Evening Star quilt block suggests a familiar industry logo. The sloping outlines of ancient mountains form the background. The old maxim—"A straight line is a line of duty; a curved line is one of beauty"—aptly describes this quilt.

Finished Size: 51⅜" x 54"
Perimeter: 210¾"
Blocks: 1 large star pentagon
      5 small star pentagons

**Fabric Requirements:**

| | |
|---|---|
| Silver metallic | 1 yard |
| Lavender | ⅞ yard |
| Rose | ½ yard |
| Assorted blues and greens | 4 yards total |
| Backing | 3⅜ yards |
| Blue for binding | ¾ yard |

**Pieces to Cut\*:**

| | |
|---|---|
| OP34 | 25 silver metallic |
| OP35 | 5 silver metallic |
| Q28 | 25 silver metallic |
| Q29 | 5 silver metallic |
| T7 | 25 lavender |
| T38 | 5 rose |

\* Refer to Steps 2–3 to cut remaining pieces.

**Quilt Construction:**

**1.** Follow quilt diagram to make 1 large star pentagon and 5 small star pentagons. Set aside.

**2.** To make full-size templates for flowing background, refer to Making Curved Templates, page 120. Draw a 51⅜" x 54" block on gridded freezer paper. (To make a sheet of paper large enough for pattern, overlap ends of paper and iron to make them adhere.) Referring to measurements on quilt diagram, draw large pentagon on block. Use flexible curve to draw curves as desired across entire block. Number templates in sequential order (the order in which you will join them). Indicate color and mark notches across curved seam lines. Cut out templates.

**3.** Iron numbered templates to wrong side of fabrics, referring to photograph for color placement or using colors of your choice. Cut out pieces, adding seam allowances. Extend notches and mark corners on seam allowances. Pin pieces together at corners and notches, remove freezer paper, and stitch.

**4.** Find midpoint of each 33⅜" side of pentagon and transfer 5 small pentagon measurements to these sides. Measure ¼" inside these and mark. Cut out pentagons on inside lines to form openings. Clip corners of openings. Set pentagons into opening.\*\*

**5.** Use same method as in Step 4 to set large star pentagon in place.\*\*

**6.** Layer backing, right side down; batting; and top, right side up. Quilt as shown in photograph or as desired. Bind quilt with blue fabric. Make and attach a casing to back of quilt for hanging.

\*\*An alternate method for piecing this quilt is to leave flowing background intact and appliqué large and small pentagons in place. Then cut away background fabric from behind pentagons, leaving ¼" seam allowance.

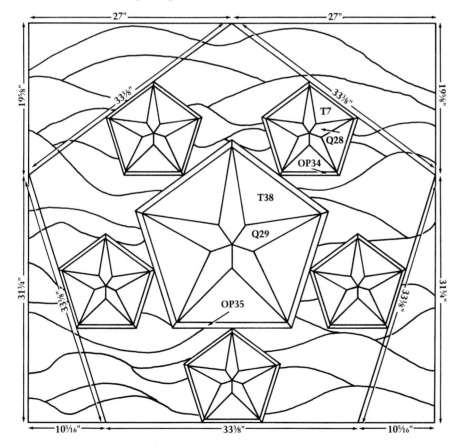

# Pastel Paisley Star

This and the remainder of the quilts in this chapter are part of more than 90 framed quilts that have come from all across the state of North Carolina to warm the walls of the obstetrics and gynecology unit of Duke University Hospital. It is an honor to be a part of this program to bring art into the hospital for the benefit of patients and their families, as well as the hospital workers.

Finished Size: 26" x 26"
Perimeter: 104"
Block: 1 (20"-square) Star block

**Fabric Requirements:**

| | |
|---|---|
| Rose print | ¼ yard |
| Paisley | ¾ yard |
| Assorted pastel prints | 1¼ yards |
| Backing | 1 yard |
| Fabric for binding | ½ yard |

**Pieces to Cut:**

| | |
|---|---|
| C1 | 1 rose print |
| OP19 | 8 light print |
| Q36 | 8 paisley |
| S3 | 4 rose print |
| | 44 assorted print |
| S10 | 8 rose print |
| | 80 assorted print |
| T31 | 16 assorted print |
| 1½" x 24½" border strip | |
| | 4 paisley |

**Quilt Construction:**

1. Referring to quilt diagram and photograph for color placement, arrange 16 assorted S10 squares into pieced block, placing rose square in 1 corner. Note how color arrangement forms stairstep pattern. Join squares. Repeat 3 times for 4 blocks.
2. Referring to quilt diagram and photograph for color placement, arrange 6 S10 squares and 4 T31 triangles into a pieced triangle. As in Step 1, note the stairstep pattern and place rose triangle at inside point of pieced triangle. Join pieces. Repeat 3 times for 4 pieced triangles.
3. Follow quilt diagram to piece center star, first joining OP19 pieces to Q36 pieces, stopping and backstitching at each corner dot. Then set in C1 circle.
4. Join stairstep triangles and then squares to pieced star.
5. Join paisley border strips to quilt, mitering corners.
6. Join assorted print and rose print S3 squares as shown in quilt diagram and photograph to make outer border. Join border to quilt.
7. Quilt as shown in photograph or as desired. Bind quilt with binding. Stretch on wooden frame for hanging.

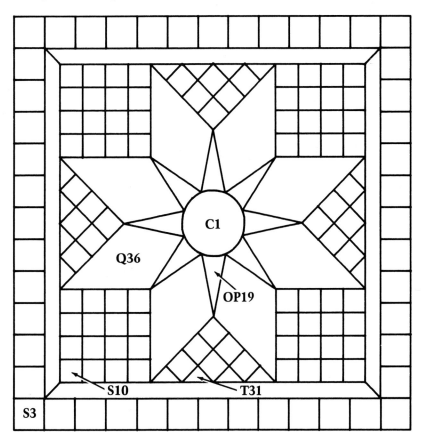

# Split Star Variation

Splitting this simple star into dynamic shades of aqua creates movement—as if the star were turning silently within its black calico frame.

Finished Size: 28" x 28"
Perimeter: 112"
Block: 1 (12"-square) Split Star block

**Fabric Requirements:**

| | |
|---|---|
| Dk. aqua print | ⅜ yard |
| Lt. aqua print | ⅜ yard |
| Peach print | ½ yard |
| Black print | ¼ yard |
| Lt. floral print | ⅜ yard |
| Med. aqua print | ¼ yard |
| Backing | 1 yard |
| Fabric for binding | ½ yard |

**Pieces to Cut:**

| | |
|---|---|
| Q2 | 8 black print |
| S5 | 1 lt. floral print |
| T9 | 4 dk. aqua print |
| T15 | 4 lt. floral print |
| T53 | 16 peach print* |
| T57 | 8 lt. aqua print |
| T58 | 8 dk. aqua print |
| 1½" x 22½" strip | 4 black print |
| 1" x 23½" strip | 4 lt. aqua print |
| 2½" x 27½" strip | 4 lt. floral print |
| 1" x 28½" strip | 4 peach print |
| 1½" x 30½" strip | 4 med. aqua print |
| 1¼" x 12½" strip | 4 black print |

*Reverse template for half the pieces.

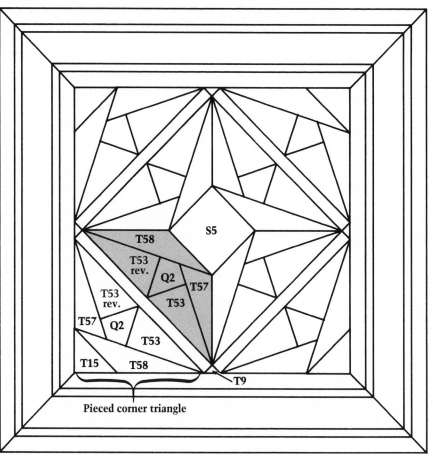

Pieced corner triangle

**Quilt Construction:**

**1.** Following shaded area of quilt diagram, join 1 Q2, 2 T53 triangles, 1 T57, and 1 T58. Repeat 3 times for 4 units. Join these units to S5 as shown in diagram, stopping at corner dots to allow for mitered angles, to complete Split Star block.

**2.** Join 2 (1¼" x 12½") black print strips to opposite sides of Split Star block. Join 1 dk. aqua print T9 triangle to each end of remaining 2 (1¼" x 12½") black print strips. Join strips to the remaining sides of Split Star block.

**3.** Following quilt diagram, make 4 pieced corner triangles. Join corner triangles to Split Star block.

**4.** Refer to quilt diagram and join borders, mitering all corners.

**5.** Quilt as shown in photograph or as desired. Bind quilt with binding. Stretch on wooden frame to hang.

# Lavender Love

Repetition breeds content! Exotic though it appears, this overlapping star is easy to make using a repeating, pinwheel-type sequence. This miniature version of the *Manteca Ribbons* quilt takes advantage of pre-printed striped fabric for its points. The possibilities for varied fabric arrangements here are many!

Finished Size: 27" x 27"
Perimeter: 108"
Blocks: 1 (16"-square) Star block

## Fabric Requirements:

| | |
|---|---|
| Dk. lavender print | ⅜ yard |
| Med. lavender print | ⅛ yard |
| Lt. lavender print | ⅛ yard |
| Med. green print | ⅜ yard |
| Green stripe | ½ yard |
| Lt. green print | ¼ yard |
| Large floral print | ¼ yard |
| Small black floral print | ⅛ yard |
| Black print | ¼ yard |
| Backing | 1 yard |
| Fabric for binding | ½ yard |

## Pieces to Cut:

| | |
|---|---|
| P6 | 8 lt. lavender print |
| P7 | 16 dk. lavender print |
| | 8 lt. lavender print |
| | 16 green stripe |
| | 8 med. green print |
| | 8 large floral print |
| Q23 | 4 green stripe |
| | 8 med. green print* |
| Q25 | 4 green stripe |
| S3 | 4 med. lavender print |
| S11 | 8 lt. lavender print |
| | 1 large floral print |
| T15 | 16 small black floral print |
| T64 | 12 dk. lavender print |
| 2" x 22½" border strip | |
| | 4 black print |

*Reverse template for half the pieces.

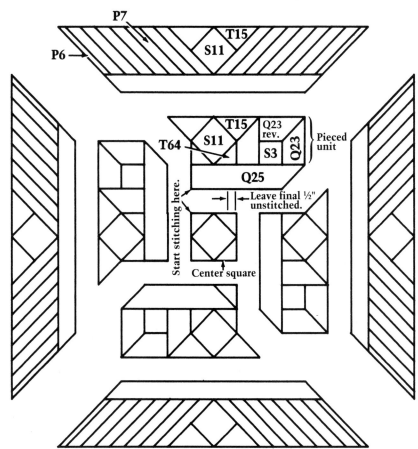

## Quilt Construction:

1. Following quilt diagram and photograph, make center star block.
2. Join remaining S11 and T15 pieces to make 4 triangles for outer border as shown in quilt diagram. Follow quilt diagram to join P6 and P7 pieces for outer border. Join pieced border units to triangles. Join inner border strips to pieced border units. Attach borders to quilt.
3. Quilt as shown in photograph.
4. Bind quilt with fabric. Stretch on wooden frame for hanging.

### Piecing Suggestion

*To complete piecing quilt top, join 1 pieced unit to top of square, leaving final ½" of seam unstitched. Proceed counterclockwise to join remaining 3 pieced units to center square. Join borders, mitering corners.*

# Car Star Variation

No two blocks alike, this quilt is a simple but happy version of the more advanced Car Star design. This one requires only a little concentration for a perfect block layout.

Finished Size: 28¼" x 29½"
Perimeter: 115½"
Blocks: 4 Star Pentagon blocks

## Fabric Requirements:

| | |
|---|---|
| Lt. floral print | 1¼ yards |
| Black print | ¼ yard |
| Yellow print | ¼ yard |
| Rose print | ¼ yard |
| Blue print | ¼ yard |
| Purple print | ¼ yard |
| Backing | 1 yard |
| Lt. floral print for binding | ½ yard |

## Pieces to Cut:

| | |
|---|---|
| OP34 | 4 black print |
| | 4 purple print |
| | 4 yellow print |
| | 4 blue print |
| | 4 rose print |
| Q28 | 8 black print |
| | 3 purple print |
| | 3 yellow print |
| | 3 blue print |
| | 3 rose print |
| S3 | 1 purple print |
| | 1 yellow print |
| | 1 blue print |
| | 1 rose print |
| T7 | 20 lt. floral print |
| T30 | 8 lt. floral print* |
| T68 | 4 lt. floral print* |
| | 1 purple print** |
| | 1 yellow print |
| | 1 blue print** |
| | 1 rose print |
| 2½" x 26" strip | 2 lt. floral print |
| 2½" x 24¾" strip | 2 lt. floral print |

*Reverse template for half the pieces.
**Reverse template.

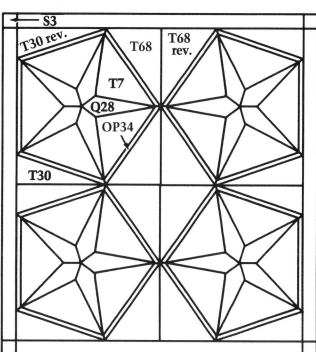

## Quilt Construction:

**1.** Referring to quilt diagram and photograph for color placement, make 4 star pentagon blocks.
**2.** Continuing to refer to photograph for color placement, join blocks, 2 across and 2 down.
**3.** Join 1 (2½" x 26") strip to top and 1 to bottom of quilt.
**4.** Join 1 S3 square to each end of each 2½" x 24¾" strip. Join pieced strips to sides of quilt top.
**5.** Quilt as shown in photograph or as desired. Bind with lt. floral print. Stretch on wooden frame for hanging.

# JUST FOR PATCHFUN

Give your imagination free rein and unleash the inspiration for your own patchwork art.

*House Exchange Program*

# House Exchange Program

Sheila Scawen and several of her quilting friends in England joined my Freedom Escape quilt class in a block exchange to create this whimsical quilt.

Finished Size: 83" x 101"
Perimeter: 368"
Blocks: 20 (15"-square) House
blocks

## Fabric Requirements:

| | |
|---|---|
| Assorted prints and solids | 2¾ yards total |
| Blue pindot | 2¼ yards |
| Border print | 3 yards |
| Backing | 6½ yards |
| Fabric for binding | ⅞ yard |

## Pieces to Cut:

House block triangle*

| | |
|---|---|
| | 80 blue pindot |
| 3½" x 15½" strip | 25 blue pindot |
| 3½" x 75½" strip | 6 blue pindot |
| 4½" x 79½" strip | 2 border print |
| 4½" x 97½" strip | 2 border print |

*See Step 1.

## Quilt Construction:

**1.** To make house block triangle template, draw a 2³⁄₁₆" x 12¹³⁄₁₆" x 13" right triangle. Add ¼" seam allowances.
**2.** Design 20 (13½") house block center squares from drawings, photographs, or from your imagination. Use freezer paper (see Gridded Freezer Paper as a Creative Tool, page 120) to make templates for house blocks. Cut out pieces and make 13½"

squares. Join 13½" edges of blue pindot triangles to edges of house blocks to tilt houses and to increase block size to 15½" (see quilt diagram for triangle placement).
**3.** Follow quilt diagram to join 3½" x 15½" sashing strips to opposite sides of blocks, creating 5 rows of 4 blocks each. Join rows with 3½" x 75½" sashing strips. Join remaining 3½" x 75½" strips to top and bottom of quilt (see quilt diagram).
**4.** Join border-print strips to edges of quilt as shown in quilt diagram.
**5.** Quilt as desired. Bind.

## Cozy Construction:

**1.** Copy a 16" x 19" house block from a photograph or draw your own design. Use freezer paper to make templates for house block (see Gridded Freezer Paper as a Creative Tool, page 120). Cut pieces from assorted prints and solids, adding ¼" seam allowance, and make block.
**2.** Cut silver cloth and 2 pieces of batting to match house block. Layer silver cloth, right side down; batting; and house block, right side up. Baste raw edges to secure all layers.
**3.** Hand-quilt house block as desired.
**4.** Enlarge Tea Set pattern on page 128 onto gridded freezer paper or draw your own design. Cut out templates.

Iron
side
addin
applic
and pr
a 16½
print.
(See A
further
appliqu
**5.** Cut s
batting t
Layer
batting; a
up. Baste
secure all l
at 1½" int
**6.** Make a

### Bright Idea!
*Do you have an accumulation of odd-sized blocks looking for a special setting? Add borders to enlarge them to a uniform size. Then tilt them by adding triangles as shown in House Exchange Program.*

# Tea

This tea...
pot, but th...
from silver...
tarnishing.

To person...
create a piec...
one side and...
pattern on th...

# Quilting 'Round the Clock

Possible variations of the snowflake concept used in the center of this quilt are endless. The appliqué is similar to Hawaiian motifs inspired by nature. *Quilting 'Round the Clock* symbolizes what comes naturally to all quilt lovers—quilting any time of day or night.

Finished Size: 36" x 36"
Perimeter: 144"
Blocks: 20 (6"-square) Going My Way
       blocks
      1 (22"-square) appliqué block

**Fabric Requirements:**

| | |
|---|---|
| White | 1 yard |
| Black | 1⅛ yards |
| Rose | ⅜ yard |
| Apricot | ⅜ yard |
| Teal | ⅜ yard |
| Blue | ⅜ yard |
| Backing | 1⅛ yards |
| Black for binding | ⅝ yard |

**Pieces to Cut:**

| | |
|---|---|
| S2 | 20 rose |
| | 20 apricot |
| | 20 teal |
| | 20 blue |
| T31 | 80 white |
| | 80 black |
| T63 | 20 rose |
| | 20 apricot |
| | 20 teal |
| | 20 blue |
| T65 | 20 rose |
| | 20 apricot |
| | 20 teal |
| | 20 blue |
| 22½"-square | 1 white |
| | 1 black |
| 1½" x 26½" strip | 4 black |

**Quilt Construction:**

1. To make appliqué pattern, cut a 22" square of freezer paper. Fold paper diagonally into quarters. Then fold in half to form a triangle. Use tracing paper to transfer pattern to folded freezer paper, placing edges on folds as indicated on pattern. Cut out pattern along outline.

2. For hand appliqué (see Step 3 for machine appliqué), unfold freezer paper pattern and iron to wrong side of 22½" square of black fabric. Cut out appliqué, adding ¼" seam allowance. Turn under seam allowance and press. Peel away freezer paper. Baste appliqué to 22½" white fabric square. Hand-appliqué. Join 1½" x 26½" border strips to sides of block, mitering corners. Set aside.

3. For machine appliqué, unfold freezer paper pattern and iron to right side of 22½" square of black fabric. With right sides up, pin black square to top of 22½" white square.

Machine-stitch near edge of freezer paper around entire design. Remove freezer paper. Trim appliqué near stitched line. Place a piece of lightweight paper underneath white fabric for stability and satin-stitch edges of appliqué, covering straight stitches. Remove paper. Cut away white fabric from behind black appliqué, leaving ¼" seam allowance. Join border strips to appliquéd square as in Step 2. Set aside.

4. Following block diagram and photograph for placement, make 20 Going My Way blocks.

5. Join blocks to make 2 (4-block) strips and 2 (6-block) strips. Referring to photograph, join 4-block strips to opposite sides of appliqué block, then 6-block strips to remaining sides.

6. Quilt as shown in photograph or as desired. Bind with black fabric.

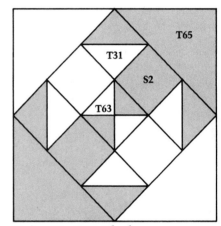

**Going My Way Block**

---

### Bright Idea!
*Use the folded snowflake technique to create appliqué designs of your own. Use a silhouette of your favorite pet, a flower, or a pretty design traced from a book. Remember that one paper fold will give you two repeats (one mirror image) of your design; two folds will give you four repeats; four folds will give you eight repeats; and so on.*

# Love Knot
## with Lap-It-Up-Again Border

A ... and a
mys...
*Kno*...
is a...
fou...

F...
P...
B...

**Quilt Construction:**
...block diagrams to make 8 A
...to pho-
...ollow
...gether
...freezer
...age 130
...Reverse
...maining
...cats to
...²") fabric
...dding ¼"
...ing quilt
...der strips.
...e of freezer
...hove freezer
...tched lines.
...of each cat,
...es. Join bor-
...ng corners.
...d with black

OP25         4 black print
R8         4 pink
        4 blue
        8 black print
5½" x 10½" rectangle  16 assorted solids
8½" square  2 pale pink
     2 lavender
5½" x 44½" border strip  4 black print

**Block A** — OP21, OP25, OP24, OP23, OP22

**Block B** — R8

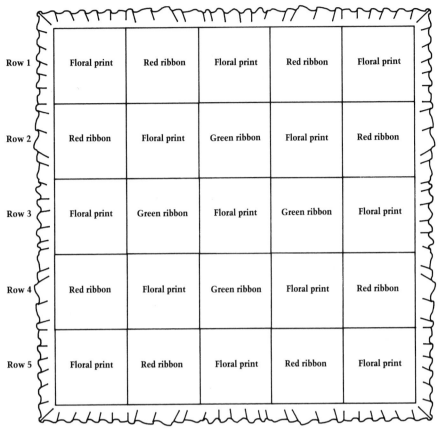

| | | | | |
|---|---|---|---|---|
| Row 1 | Floral print | Red ribbon | Floral print | Red ribbon | Floral print |
| Row 2 | Red ribbon | Floral print | Green ribbon | Floral print | Red ribbon |
| Row 3 | Floral print | Green ribbon | Floral print | Green ribbon | Floral print |
| Row 4 | Red ribbon | Floral print | Green ribbon | Floral print | Red ribbon |
| Row 5 | Floral print | Red ribbon | Floral print | Red ribbon | Floral print |

# Decorator's Cover

This quilt, designed and made by my sister, Jill Moore, uses a ribbon decorator print cut to form a trellis. If you aren't able to find the ribbon print, consider appliquéing purchased satin ribbon onto 14½-inch squares of white fabric.

Finished Size: 70" x 70" (excluding ruffle)
Perimeter: 280"
Blocks: 13 (14"-square) floral print blocks
  12 (14"-square) ribbon trellis blocks

| Material Requirements: | 45" Fabric | 60" Fabric |
|---|---|---|
| Floral print | 2¾ yards | 1½ yards |
| Red ribbon print | 3⅞ yards | 3 yards |
| Green ribbon print | 1 yard | ½ yard |
| Medium cording | 8⅝ yards | 8⅝ yards |
| Backing | 4⅜ yards | 4⅜ yards |

**Pieces to Cut:**

| | |
|---|---|
| 14½" square | 13 floral print |
| | 4 green ribbon print |
| | 8 red ribbon print |
| | 25 backing |
| 6½"-wide strip | 11⅝ yards red ribbon print |
| 1¾"-wide bias strip | 8⅝ yards red ribbon print |

## Quilt Construction:

**1.** Cut 25 (14½") squares of batting. Stack backing, right side down; batting; and print square, right side up. Machine-quilt block, following design in fabric. (See Machine Quilting, page 121.) Repeat to quilt remaining blocks. Follow quilt diagram to join blocks to form rows; then join rows. (See Lap-Quilting Connections, page 121.)

**2.** Make 8⅝ yards of corded piping, using cording and 1¾"-wide bias strip. Trim seam allowance to ½". With right sides facing and raw edges aligned, baste piping around outer edge of quilt top layer only. (Do not baste piping to batting and backing.)

**3.** To make ruffle, fold 6½"-wide strip in half lengthwise with wrong sides facing. Gather to fit perimeter of quilt. With right sides facing and raw edges aligned, baste ruffle around edges of quilt top only. Using ½" seam allowance, sew ruffle and cording to quilt top only.

**4.** Trim ½" from outer edges of batting. Fold seam allowances of quilt top and backing to inside of quilt. Slipstitch backing to quilt top along folded edges.

### Bright Idea!

*Don't forget the decorator section of your fabric store when choosing quilt fabrics. The florals, stripes, picture prints, and even plaids offer a whole new world of patchwork possibilities.*

# TIPS AND TRICKS

Turn the following pages to find new ideas and techniques to help you grow in your craft and attain your quilting aspirations.

*Modern Moon Over the Mountain*

# Modern Moon Over the Mountain

Introducing curves into quilt designs can update traditional patterns and give them a personal touch. This contemporary version of the *Moon Over the Mountain* quilt is part of the Duke University Hospital collection. The design relies on the flexible curve to make the one-of-a-kind curved background. See Making Curved Templates on page 120 for more about the flexible curve.

Finished Size: 27" x 27"
Perimeter: 108"
Blocks: 1 (18"-square) Moon Over the Mountain block
    32 (3"-square) Mini-mountain border blocks

## Fabric Requirements:
Assorted light and dark prints*

| | |
|---|---|
| | 1 yard total |
| Black print | ¾ yard |
| Backing | ⅞ yard |
| Fabric for binding | ½ yard |

*See photograph for color suggestions.

## Pieces to Cut:

| | |
|---|---|
| T4 | 32 dark print |
| | 96 light print |
| 2" x 23½" strip | 4 black print |

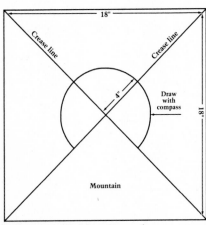

**Diagram: Making Templates**

## Quilt Construction:

**1.** To make templates for Moon Over the Mountain block, cut an 18" square of gridded freezer paper. Fold paper to create 2 diagonal creases (see diagram at left). Unfold square. Use a straightedge to draw mountain (bottom triangle) on gridded side of paper.
**2.** Place the point of the compass at apex of the mountain. Draw a circle arc with 4" radius for moon, beginning and ending the arc at the sides of the mountain.
**3.** Refer to Making Curved Templates, page 120. Using flexible curve, draw curved lines across square horizontally through sky, moon, and mountain (see quilt diagram). Code templates for orderly piecing.
**4.** Cut out templates and press shiny side of freezer paper to wrong side of fabric. Cut out pieces, adding ¼" seam allowances. Pin ends and midpoints of seam allowances.
**5.** Piece block, removing freezer paper each time a new curve is sewn.
**6.** Join 2" x 23½" inner border strips to quilt top, mitering corners.
**7.** Refer to photograph and quilt diagram to piece 32 border blocks. Join blocks in 2 rows of 7 and 2 rows of 9. Join borders to quilt top.
**8.** Quilt as desired. Bind with bias binding. Stretch on wooden frame for hanging.

# Lap-Quilting Update

On the following pages, I will discuss many of the techniques used to make the quilts in this book. Some are updated versions of traditional methods; some are my own discoveries. I hope they will help you turn *your* bright ideas into unique and fabulous quilts.

## Gridded Freezer Paper as a Creative Tool

Ever since I discovered that freezer paper could be used as an aid in machine piecing, new doors of creative piecework have opened for me. With my gridded freezer paper, which I call Grid Grip, I can make instant templates. Iron the templates onto the wrong side of the fabric and cut them out, adding ¼" seam allowance. I often leave the Grid Grip templates in place as stitching guides. The templates can then be easily peeled away—to be used again and again.

Grid Grip is useful not only for making templates. The ¼" grid that covers Grid Grip can be used to enlarge patterns and to place grain lines.

Note that the templates are usually ironed onto the wrong side of the fabric. That means when the design is stitched in place, the image is reversed. Therefore, designs that have a direction, such as letters and numerals, should be drawn on the shiny side of the Grid Grip. For all designs, transfer lines in pencil first. Then trace over pencil lines with a fine-point, indelible pen.

You can create a mirror image with Grid Grip without making new templates. Simply iron Grid Grip templates to the right side of the fabric instead of the wrong side.

To order my catalog that features Grid Grip and many other quilting supplies, see page 160. If you prefer, use regular freezer paper, available at most supermarkets.

Following are the techniques that I use with Grid Grip:

**Picture Strip Piecing:** This technique was used in the *Cruise and Quilt Banner*, page 52, and *Little Toot* quilt, page 24.

Transfer the design to Grid Grip. On the Grid Grip drawing, draw vertical or horizontal lines to make rows (see Diagram 1). With an indelible pen, code the design, labeling the rows A, B, C, etc., left to right. Number the templates from top to bottom and indicate color. Grain lines are built in on the grid.

Cut the Grid Grip design into vertical rows, using a rotary cutter or scissors. (Be sure to keep a copy of the whole original design for reference when piecing your design.) Next, cut 1 row at a time apart into individual templates, cutting on outlines.

Cut the fabrics into strips ½" wider than the width of the rows. Match the color-coded templates to the fabrics. Center a template on the wrong side of a strip. Press the template onto the fabric with a warm iron. Leaving 1" between templates, continue pressing the templates onto the fabrics. Cut the pieces out, with ¼" seam allowance all around each template.

With right sides facing, hold the fabric pieces to be joined toward a light source and align the edges of the

freezer paper. Using a straight stitch and matching thread, join the fabric pieces, with right sides facing, using the edges of the templates as a stitching guide and being careful not to catch the paper in the seam. With right sides facing, sew the rows together, using the templates as a stitching guide. Remove templates.

**Enlarging Patterns:** *Spotlight Dancing Spools*, page 19, and *Moonbeams Over Many Ports*, page 56, use this technique. These designs are printed on a grid. To enlarge them, use Grid Grip or draw a grid on regular freezer paper, graph paper, or plain white paper. A notation on the original (small) grid will indicate the size to make the squares. Transfer the design from the original (small) grid to the large grid, square by square.

**Making Curved Templates:** Use this technique to make the border on *The Big Ship*, page 54, the background of *Car Star*, page 94, and the *Modern Moon Over the Mountain* quilt, page 118. Templates for the wavy border and background were drawn using a flexible curve, a draftsman's tool that bends to form curves. (The flexible curve is featured in my catalog, listed on page 160.)

Bend the flexible curve into the desired shape. (Remember that the deeper or sharper the curve, the more difficult it is to sew.) Cut a piece of freezer paper the size that your finished unit will be. Place the flexible curve on the freezer paper. Trace the curve onto the paper. Lift the curve; replace it and continue as above until the desired design is complete.

Before cutting the templates apart, draw notches (as in dress patterns) on the curved lines to match the cut pieces for stitching. Code templates according to piecing sequence.

After the freezer paper template has been cut and ironed onto the fabric, extend the notch marks into the seam allowances. Clip the curves.

**Diagram 1: Picture Strip Piecing**

Match the notches and pin the fabric pieces together at the corners and midpoints. Remove the paper and stitch the seams.

**Grid Grip Templates:** Grid Grip or freezer paper can be used to make templates for any of the designs in this book. Trace the seam line onto the paper and proceed, using the paper edge as a stitching guide for straight seams and removing the paper before stitching for curved seams.

## Quilting Techniques

Old-fashioned notions such as, "A quilt is not a quilt unless it's totally handmade," are falling by the wayside. With modern inventive techniques, we can finish faster and therefore produce more, still keeping our quality at its peak.

I continue to enjoy the benefits of lap quilting. Sometimes I lap-quilt in sections, and sometimes I quilt a whole basted quilt in my lap. Each method has its merits, so today's quilter can be versatile.

Let's examine today's quilting methods and options:

**Hand Quilting:** When you are hand-quilting in a hoop or frame, quilting lines should be marked before basting. If you are quilting in small sections, basting is essential. Only limited basting is required when you are using a large frame. The frame supports the entire quilt and spreads it out fully.

When lap-quilting small sections without a frame or hoop, the hands often perform at a different angle. Here the off-hand (hand under the quilt) acts as a feeder, manipulating the layers toward the needle. Be careful not to pull the thread too taut.

**Machine Quilting:** This technique works best with small pieces such as baby quilts and wall hangings or with sectional lap quilting. I never try to duplicate hand quilting on the sewing machine. Instead I take a completely new approach, attempting to stitch quilting lines with a minimum of stopping and starting. A walking foot adapter on the machine

permits the layers of fabric to flow evenly.

Another creative technique for machine-quilting that I use is similar to darning by machine. For this technique, use a darning foot. Place the 3 layers of your quilt in a hoop. Place the area to be quilted under your needle. With the feed dogs dropped, take 1 stitch; then pull up the bobbin thread to the right side of the fabric. Holding both threads, stitch in place to lock the stitch. Now you are ready to "meander" or "loiter," quilting your desired design, moving the hoop as needed. Try to develop scribbles and patterns that are easily repeated, such as a figure 8, a leaf, or a circle. When you've finished quilting the design and you are ready to break off your thread, stop and stitch in place to lock the stitch. Before trying this on your quilt, practice your shapes on scraps.

**Hand and Machine Quilting:** A combination of hand and machine quilting on the same quilt joins the best of both worlds. When you are machine-quilting, basting threads tend to get caught in the walking or darning foot. So hand-quilt selected areas and pull out all basting threads before machine-quilting. The hand quilting then acts as a stabilizer.

**Tie Tacking:** This technique is usually associated with baby quilts, but it can work well for large quilts too. Use a long, sharp large-eyed needle and cotton yarn. With the 3 layers of the quilt pulled taut and secured in a frame, take a ¼" stitch through all layers every 5" to 6" across the quilt, leaving the yarn uncut between stitches. When the top is covered with stitches, snip the yarn halfway between stitches and tie a double knot at each stitch. Trim the ends of the yarn to about ½" or to the length desired.

## Appliqué Accents

Appliqué is the application of cutout shapes to a foundation. I use 4 different appliqué techniques in this book.

**Reverse Buttonhole or Blanket Stitch:** I used this method to machine-appliqué the moose on the *Masks, Moose, and Qupak* quilt, page 46.

This stitch is available on most modern sewing machines. Pin the figure to be appliquéd in place, set the machine for reverse buttonhole or blanket stitch, and stitch around the figure. To keep the figure from shifting during stitching, fuse the cutout to the background with fusible web first.

**Traditional Appliqué:** This method, which I used in *Quilting 'Round the Clock* on page 110, is the most common. Turn under ⅛" to ¼" on the raw edges around the figure and press or baste them. Pin the figure in place and attach it with a slipstitch. An alternative method is to pin the figure in place without turning under the raw edges. Then use your needle to turn under the edges as you stitch.

**Running Stitch:** I used this technique to appliqué the feather panels on the *UK Sampler* on page 58. Use fine matching thread and small stitches to stitch very close to the edge of the turned-under seam allowance of the appliqué figure.

**Satin Stitch:** The appliqué figure, such as a leaf in *Autumn Windows*, page 22, is cut out of freezer paper and pressed onto the right side of the fabric. Cut out the figure, adding ½" seam allowance. Place the figure on the foundation fabric and secure it with a running stitch next to the paper edge. Remove the paper and trim the fabric up to the stitching line. With lightweight paper under the foundation fabric, outline the figure with a narrow machine satin stitch (close zigzag). (Learn to adjust the width of the zigzag stitch as you come to narrow points.) Cut away foundation fabric under the figure if color shows through or if you plan to hand-quilt inside the figure.

## Lap-Quilting Connections

**Block-to-Block Connections:** With this technique, the blocks are quilted before being joined. Two steps are essential for making block-to-block connections: a) that the backing, batting, and top of all lap-quilted blocks be trimmed to the same size; and b) that at least ½" be left unquilted on the perimeter of the blocks.

After the blocks are quilted, set them together in either horizontal or vertical rows. Lay 2 blocks side by side on a flat surface, backing side up. Pin the backing and batting away from the edge on 1 block. Pin only the backing away from the edge on the other block. Stack the 2 blocks with right sides of the quilt top facing and edges and corners aligned. With the batting against the feed dogs, stitch ¼" from the edge.

Remove the pins. With the backing side up, lay the blocks out flat. Trim the batting so that the 2 pieces of batting abut. Let the backing on 1 block lie flat on top of the batting. Turn the backing on the adjoining block under ¼" and slipstitch it to the backing on the first block with quilting thread, taking care not to stitch through to the quilt top.

**Row-to-Row Connections:** Before lap-quilting, join the blocks in horizontal or vertical rows. Remember to attach any sashing and borders to the quilt top row by row so that they will be included as you quilt and will be ready for row-to-row assembly. With this technique you will be handling more material while lap-quilting than with block-to-block connections, but the technique lets you eliminate the extra connecting seams.

Join rows as in block-to-block assembly. Pinning and basting are essential for ease of handling.

**Quilt-and-Extend Method:** I used this technique when making the *UK Sampler* on page 58. The method permits you to quilt always on the perimeter section of a quilt as it grows. (Quilting all the way to the raw edge is appropriate here.)

Start by quilting the center section of the quilt. Follow Diagram 2 to attach an adjoining section as follows:

With raw edges aligned, stack the top of the new section, wrong side down; the center quilted section, top side down; the backing of the new section, right side down; and the batting of new section. (Basting the batting to the backing keeps it in place while stitching.) Baste all layers together; then with the batting against the feed dogs, stitch ¼" from the edge. Trim excess batting from the seam.

Fold the backing, top, and batting of the new section outward. Baste all layers of the new section together. Quilt. Continue with additional sections until the quilt is complete.

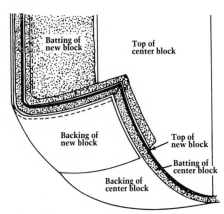

**Diagram 2: Quilt-and-Extend Method**

**Backing Accents:** This procedure, which I used on *Star Glaze*, page 34, and *Baby Buggy Boomers*, page 84, adds a touch of color to the back of the quilt to coordinate with the front. Cut 1½" strips of binding (bias or straight of the grain). With tops facing and raw edges aligned, lay the quilted rows together. With right side of binding against quilt backing and raw edges aligned, lay binding along edge of the quilted row. Pin and stitch through all layers.

Trim the batting in the seam to relieve bulk. Open quilted sections. Press binding flat over seam. Turn edge of binding under ¼" and slipstitch in place. (See Diagram 3, Figures 1 and 2).

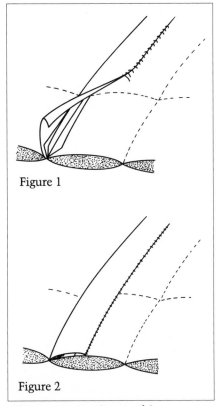

Figure 1

Figure 2

**Diagram 3: Sewing Backing Accents**

**Sew-and-Flip Method**

Sew-and-flip is my version of old-time string piecing. You'll find it used in *Baby Buggy Boomers* on page 84. You can string-piece using the bounty of your scrap bag, or plan your quilt around a color theme and buy special fabric just for that project.

Start by cutting out a foundation shape. Be sure to include seam allowances on the foundation shape. (In *Baby Buggy Boomers*, the foundation shape is a rectangle.) Cut your fabric into strips (strings). Grain lines are not important; neither is the width of the strips. But make sure that your strips are long enough to extend over the edges of the foundation piece.

With right side up, pin the first string in place across the center of your foundation shape (see Diagram 4, Figure 1). Place the second string on top of the first, with right sides facing and raw edges aligned on the edge to be stitched. (It's important to line up these edges so that a dark

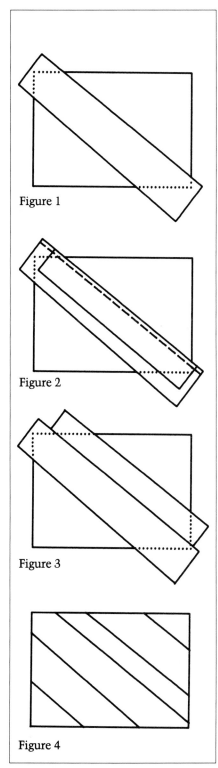

Figure 1

Figure 2

Figure 3

Figure 4

**Diagram 4: Sew-and-Flip Method**

fabric doesn't later show through a light addition.) Stitch through all layers, using a ¼" seam (see Diagram 4, Figure 2).

Flip the second piece over to reveal the right side of the fabric and press it in place (see Diagram 4, Figure 3). Continue to sew and flip, first on 1 side of the central strip and then on the other, until the entire foundation shape is covered. Trim the strings even with the foundation fabric (see Diagram 4, Figure 4).

### Continuous Bias Binding Formula

After that last stitch has been taken, the quilt is ready to be bound. I prefer a double-fold bias binding, made by sewing a bias tube for cutting continuous bias binding. In some instances, I use straight-of-the-grain binding. A standard width is 2½", pressed in half and aligned at the raw edges. The raw edges of the binding are aligned with the raw edge of the quilt top and sewn in place. Then the folded edge of the binding is turned to the back of the quilt and slipstitched in place.

Quilter Marion Snell gave me this formula for determining how big a piece of fabric is required for making bias binding for a quilt. Find the perimeter of the quilt by adding the lengths of all 4 sides. Multiply the perimeter by the desired width of the binding. Take the square root of that figure. (A calculator with a square root function is very helpful.) That figure is the size of the square of fabric required to make enough binding for your quilt. (If you prefer to use purchased binding, simply divide your perimeter by 36" for the number of yards of binding you'll need.)

To make bias binding, cut the square in half diagonally to make 2 triangles. With right sides facing and raw edges aligned, place the 2 triangles together and stitch (see Diagram 5, Figure 1). Press the seam open. Use a straightedge to mark off parallel lines the desired width of the binding (see Diagram 5, Figure 2).

Fold the parallelogram in half crosswise, right sides facing. Form a tube by joining the raw edges marked

Seam 2 (see Diagram 5, Figure 3). As you align the edges, extend a Seam 2 point past its natural matching edge by the distance of the width of the bias strip. Stitch a ¼" seam. Press the seam open.

Cut the binding in a continuous strip, starting with the protruding point and following marked lines around the tube. Fold the strip in half lengthwise and press it.

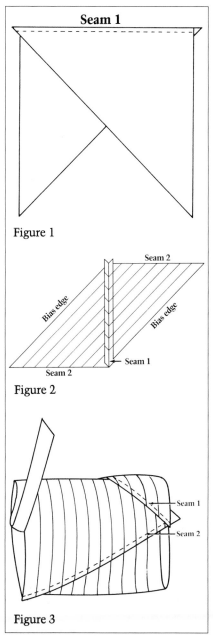

Seam 1

Figure 1

Figure 2

Figure 3

**Diagram 5: Continuous Bias Binding Formula**

# PATTERNS and TEMPLATES

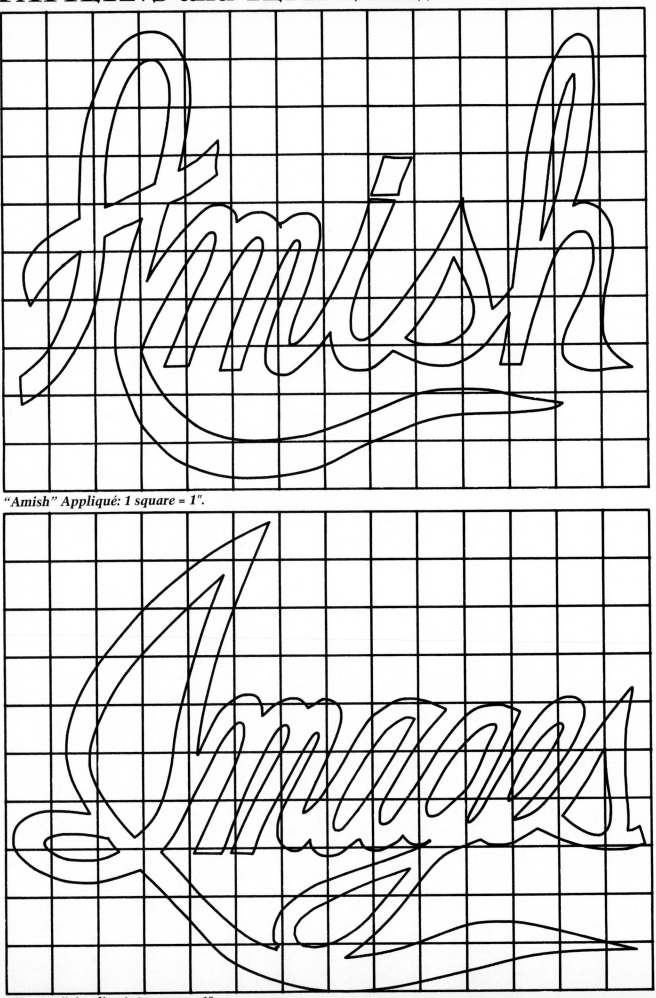

*"Amish" Appliqué: 1 square = 1".*

*"Images" Appliqué: 1 square = 1".*

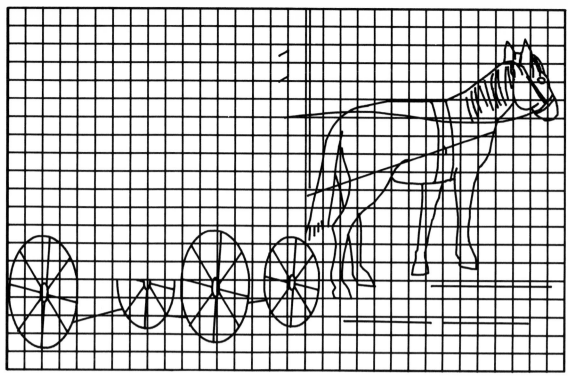

**Horse and Buggy Quilting Pattern:**
**1 square = 1″.**

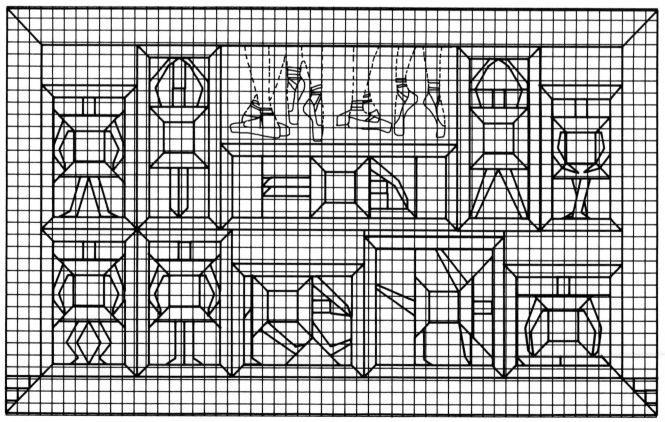

**Spotlight Dancing Spools: 1 square = 1″.**

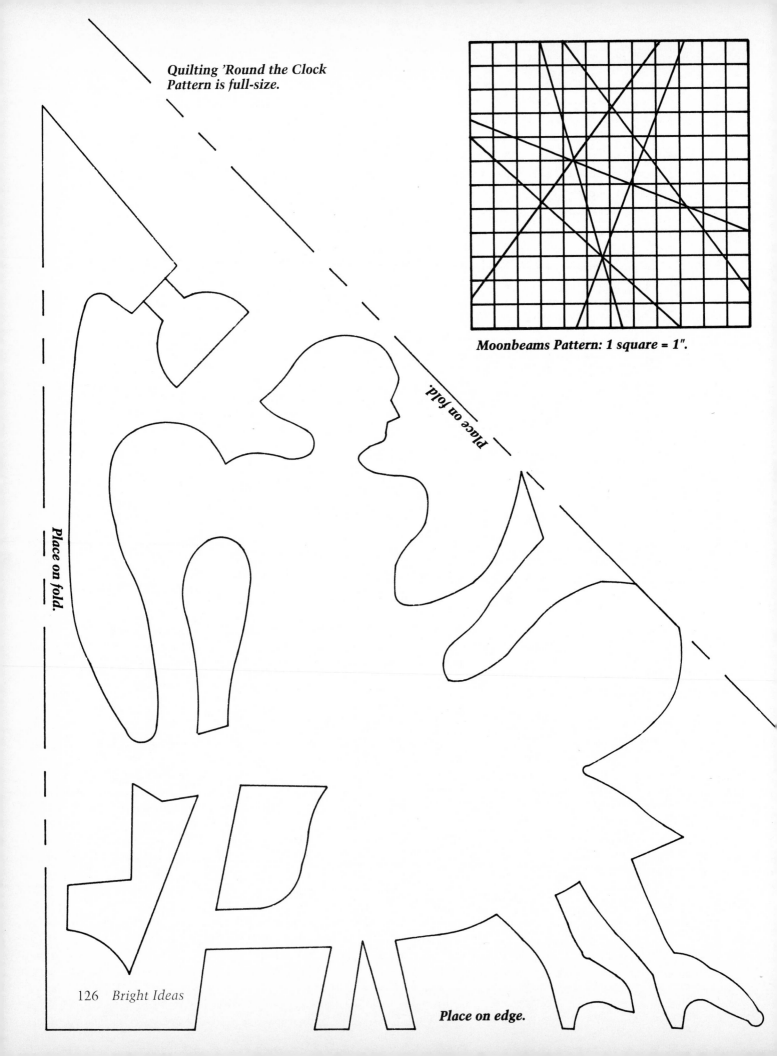

**Quilting 'Round the Clock
Pattern is full-size.**

**Moonbeams Pattern: 1 square = 1".**

Place on fold.

Place on fold.

Place on fold.

**Place on edge.**

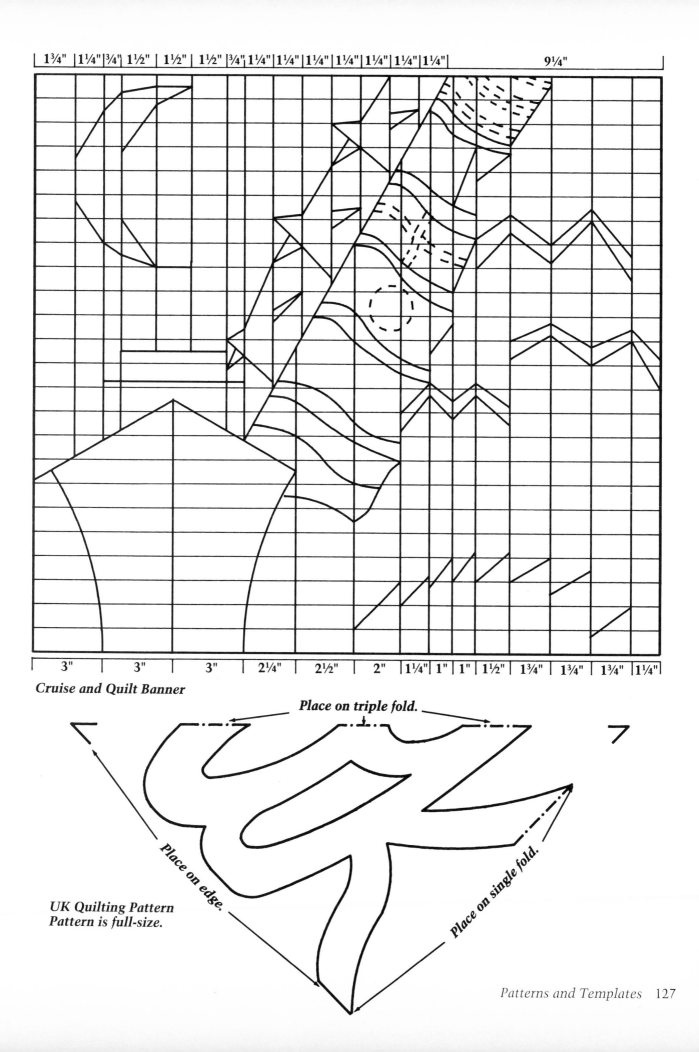

| 1¾" | 1¼" | ¾" | 1½" | 1½" | 1½" | ¾" | 1¼" | 1¼" | 1¼" | 1¼" | 1¼" | 1¼" | 1¼" | 9¼" |
|------|------|------|------|------|------|------|------|------|------|------|------|------|------|------|

| 3" | 3" | 3" | 2¼" | 2½" | 2" | 1¼" | 1" | 1" | 1½" | 1¾" | 1¾" | 1¾" | 1¼" |
|-----|-----|-----|------|------|-----|------|-----|-----|------|------|------|------|------|

**Cruise and Quilt Banner**

**Place on triple fold.**

**Place on edge.**

**Place on single fold.**

**UK Quilting Pattern**
**Pattern is full-size.**

**Moose Appliqué**
**Pattern is full-size.**

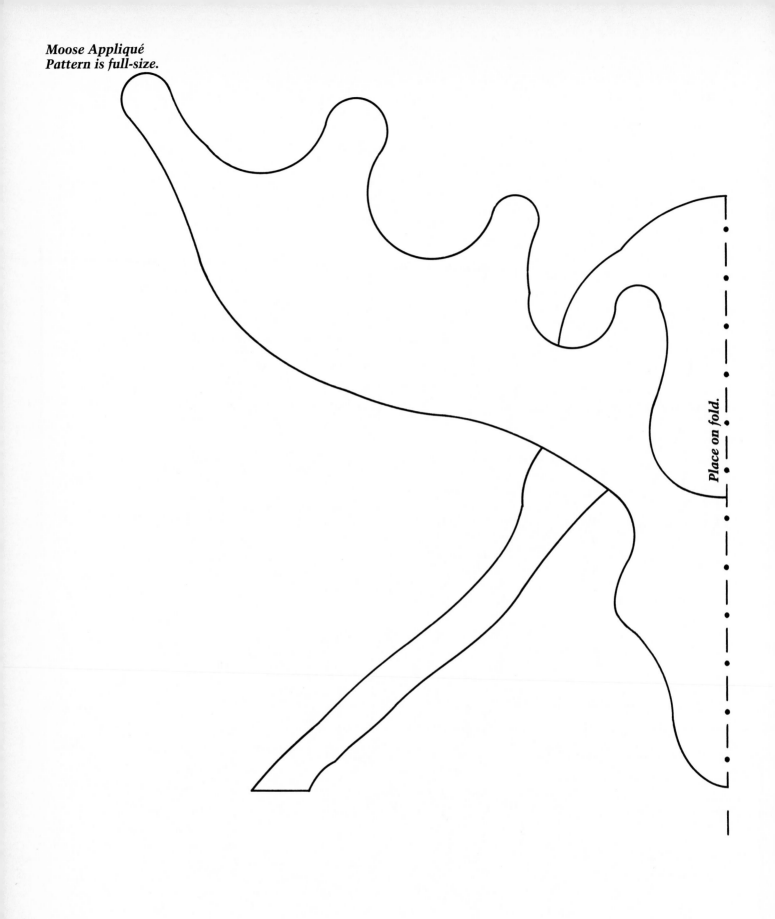

*Place on fold.*

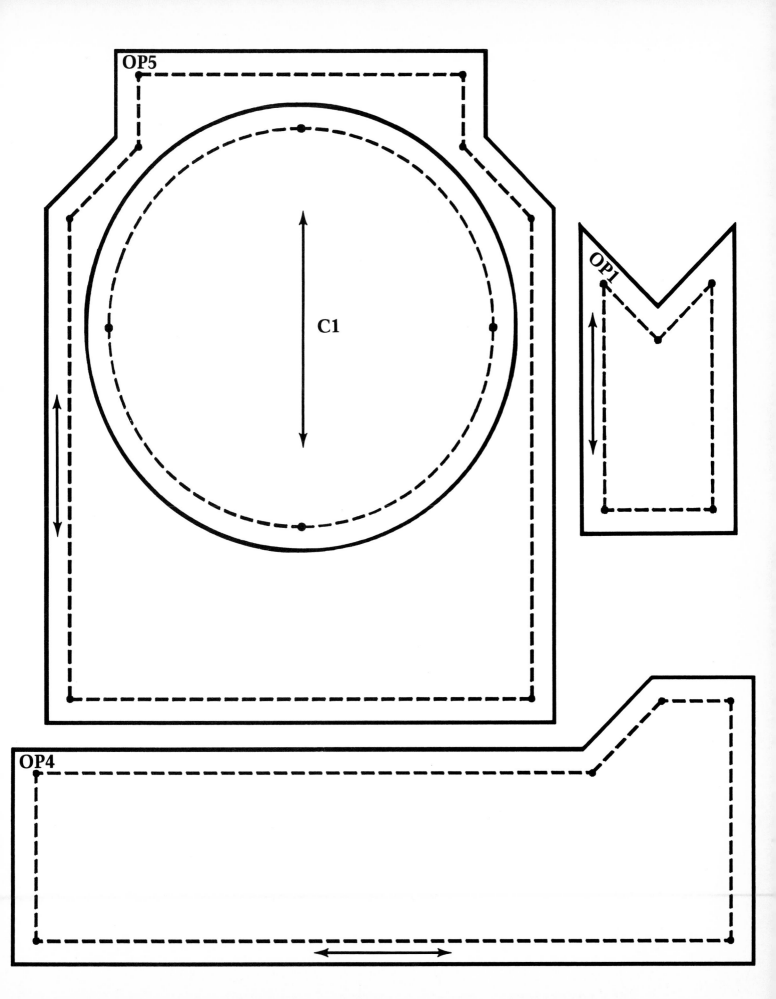

OP5

C1

OP1

OP4

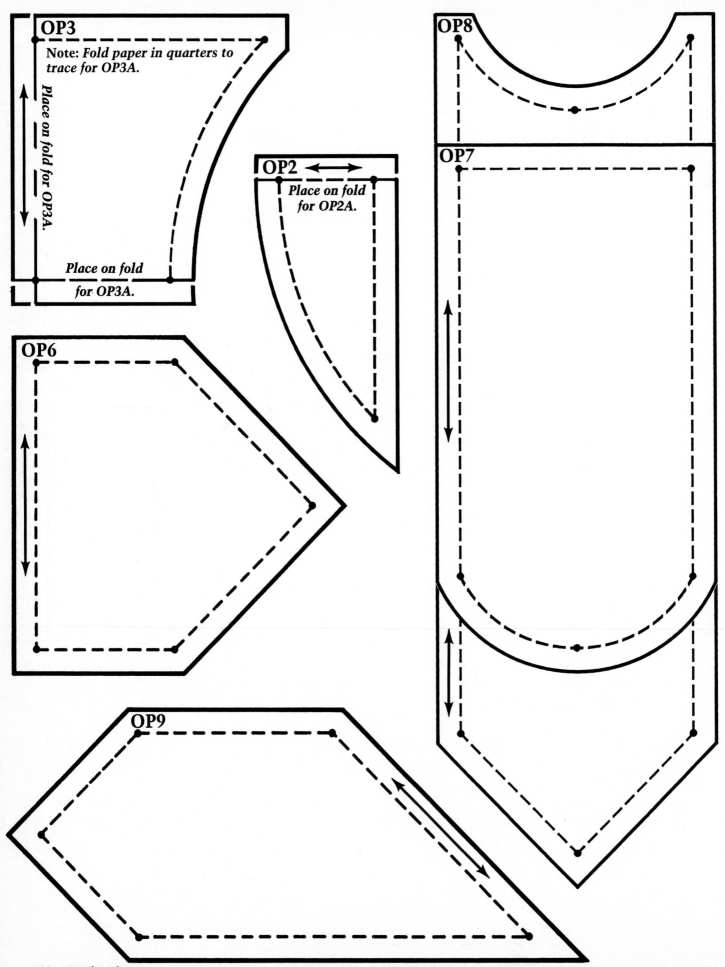

OP3

Note: *Fold paper in quarters to trace for OP3A.*

*Place on fold for OP3A.*

*Place on fold for OP3A.*

OP2

*Place on fold for OP2A.*

OP8

OP7

OP6

OP9

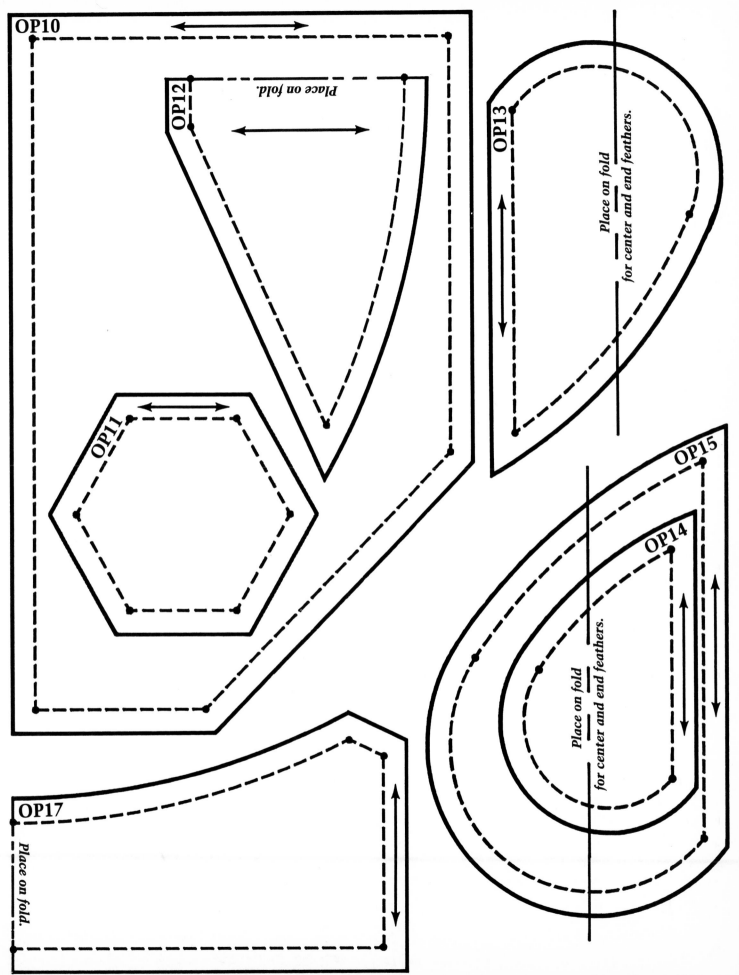

OP10

OP12

Place on fold.

OP11

OP13

Place on fold
for center and end feathers.

OP15

OP14

Place on fold
for center and end feathers.

OP17

Place on fold.

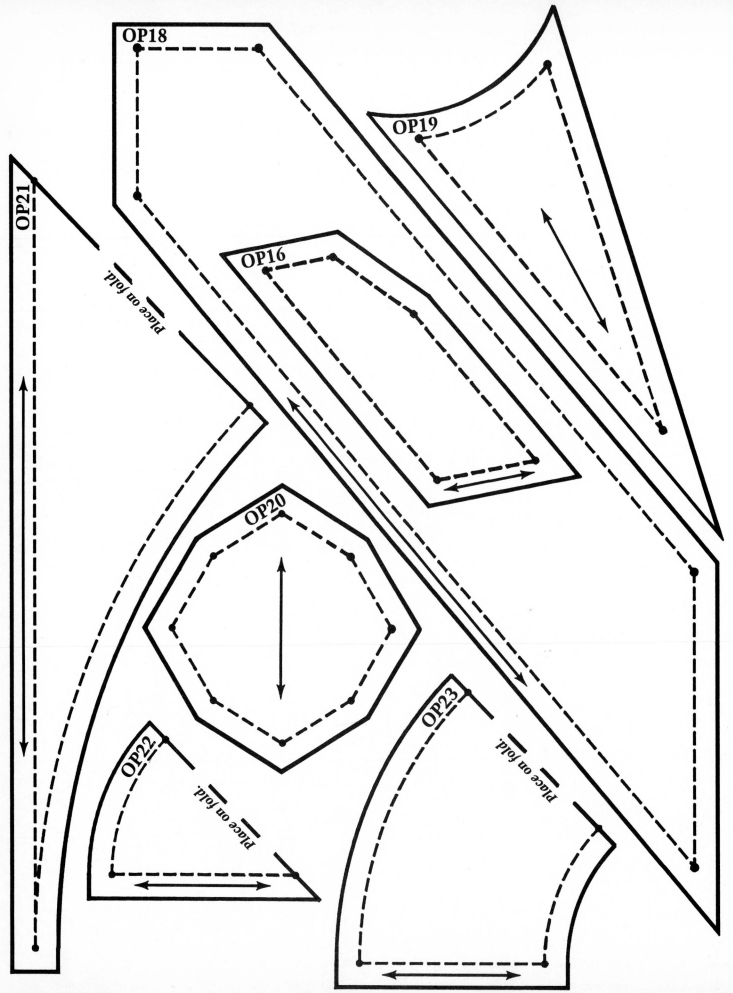

OP18

OP19

OP21

OP16

Place on fold.

OP20

OP22

OP23

Place on fold.

Place on fold.

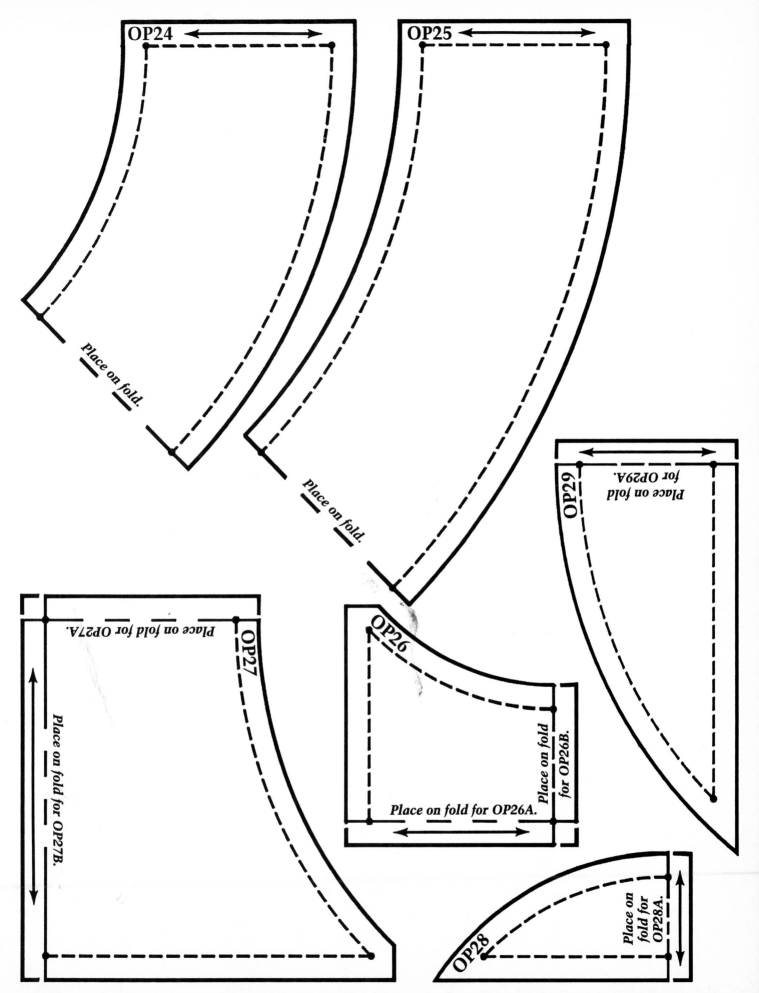

OP24 Place on fold.

OP25 Place on fold.

OP29 Place on fold for OP29A.

OP27 Place on fold for OP27A.

Place on fold for OP27B.

OP26 Place on fold for OP26A.

Place on fold for OP26B.

OP28 Place on fold for OP28A.

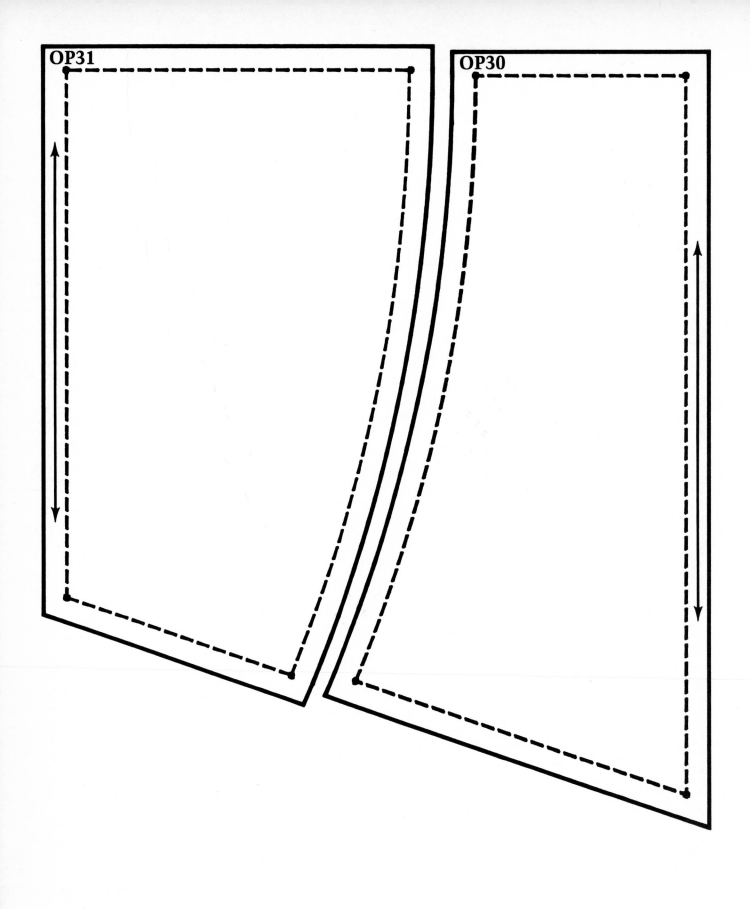

OP31

OP30

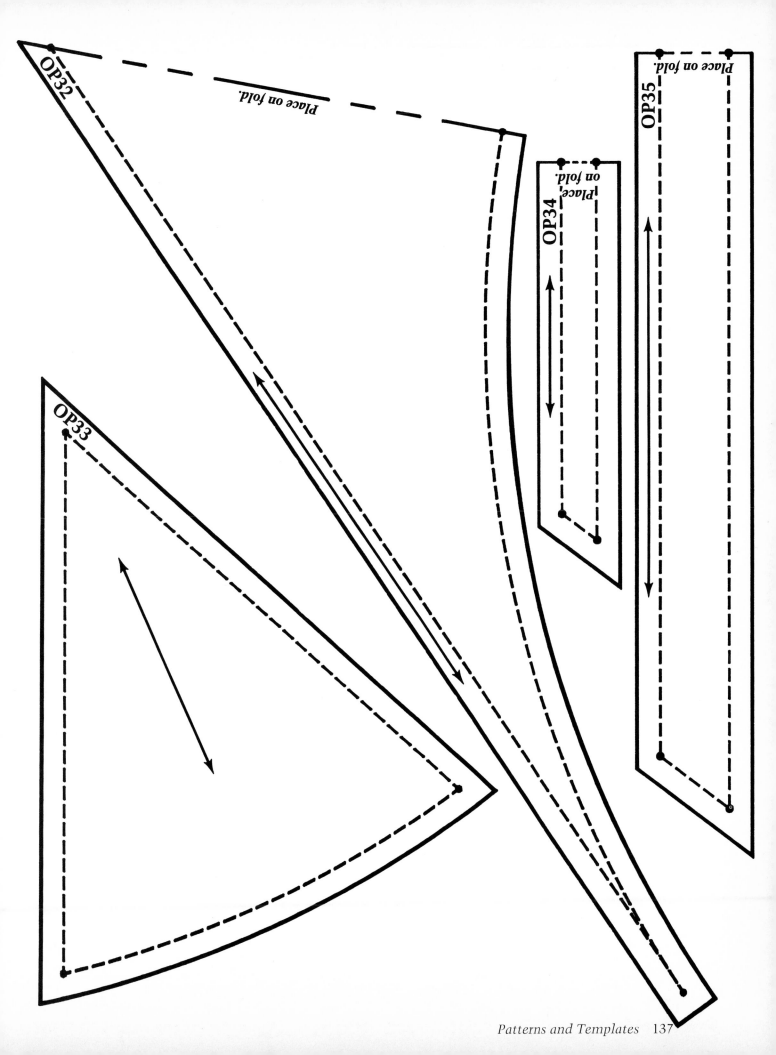

OP32

OP33

OP34

OP35

*Place on fold.*

*Place on fold.*

*Place on fold.*

*Place on fold.*

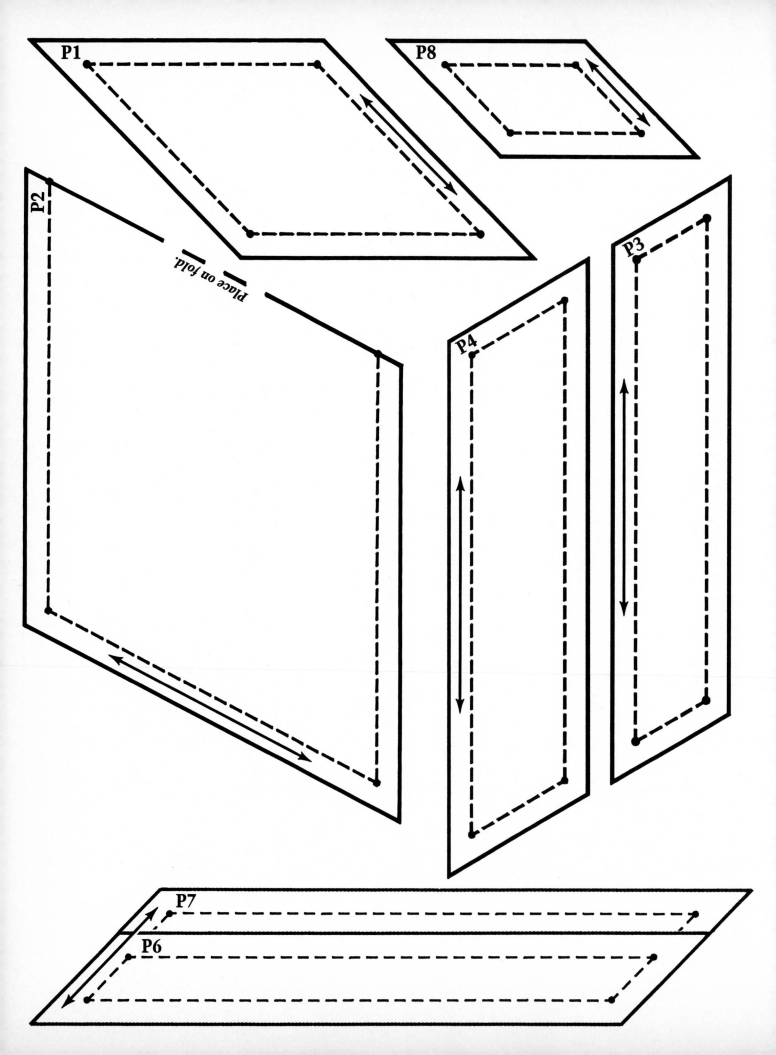

P1

P8

P2

P3

P4

*Place on fold.*

P7

P6

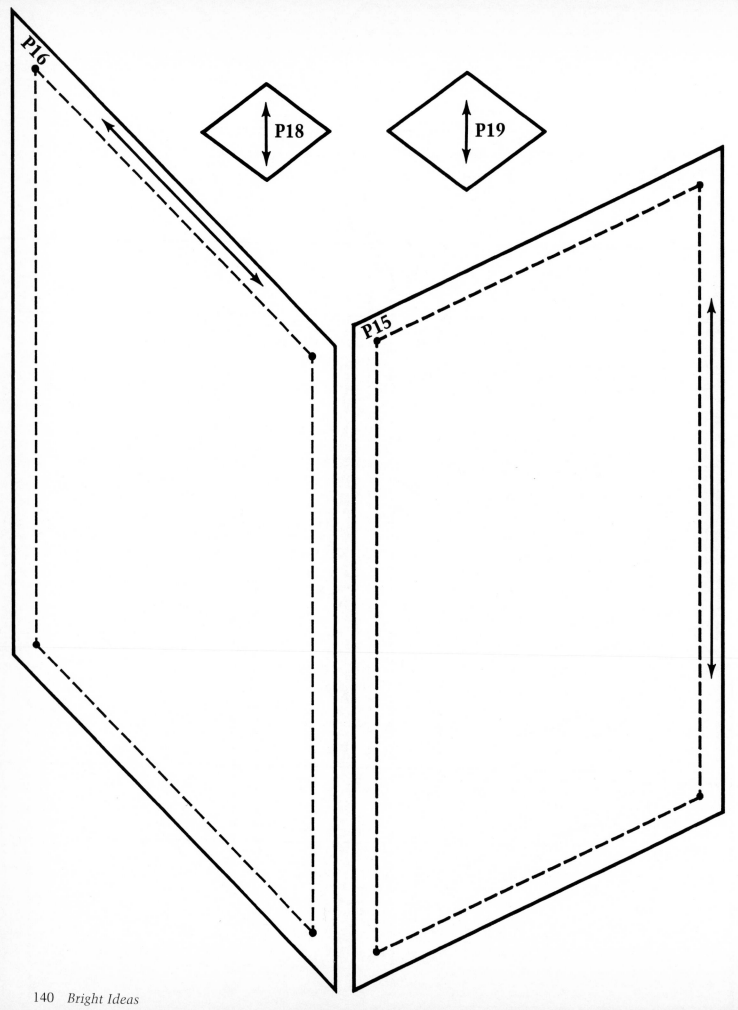

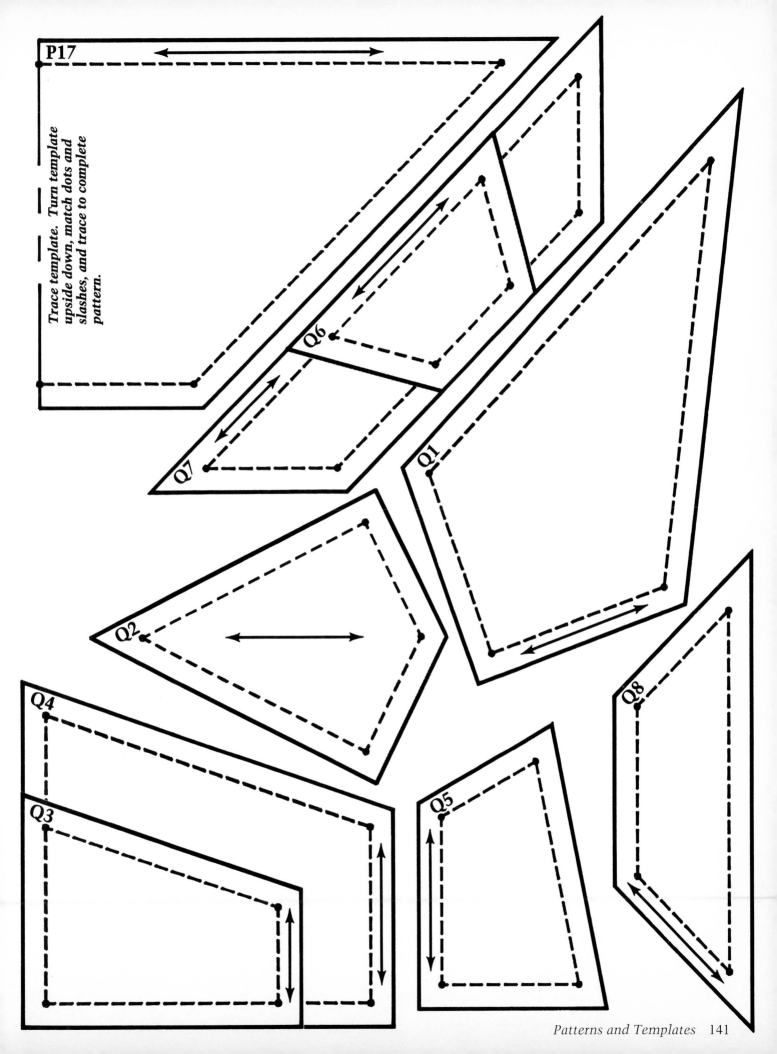

**P17**

*Trace template. Turn template upside down, match dots and slashes, and trace to complete pattern.*

Q6

Q7

Q1

Q2

Q4

Q3

Q5

Q8

Q9

Q15

*Place on fold.*

Q16

Q14

Q11

*Place on fold.*

Q13

Q12

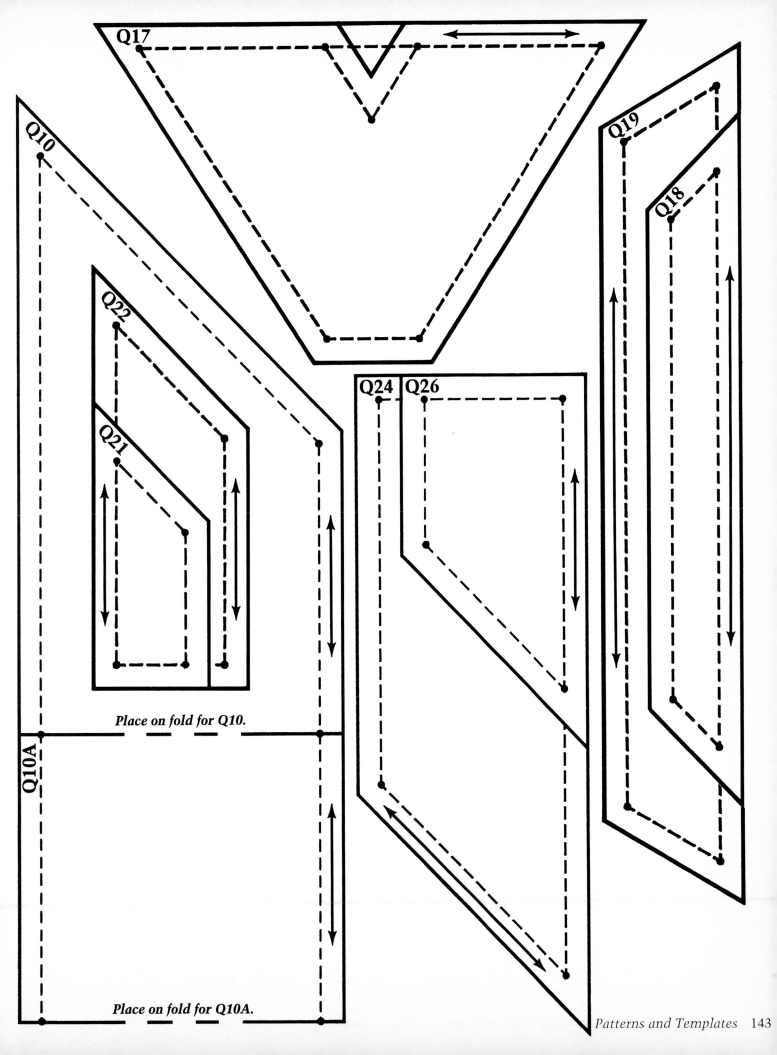

Q17

Q10

Q22

Q21

Place on fold for Q10.

Q10A

Place on fold for Q10A.

Q24 Q26

Q19

Q18

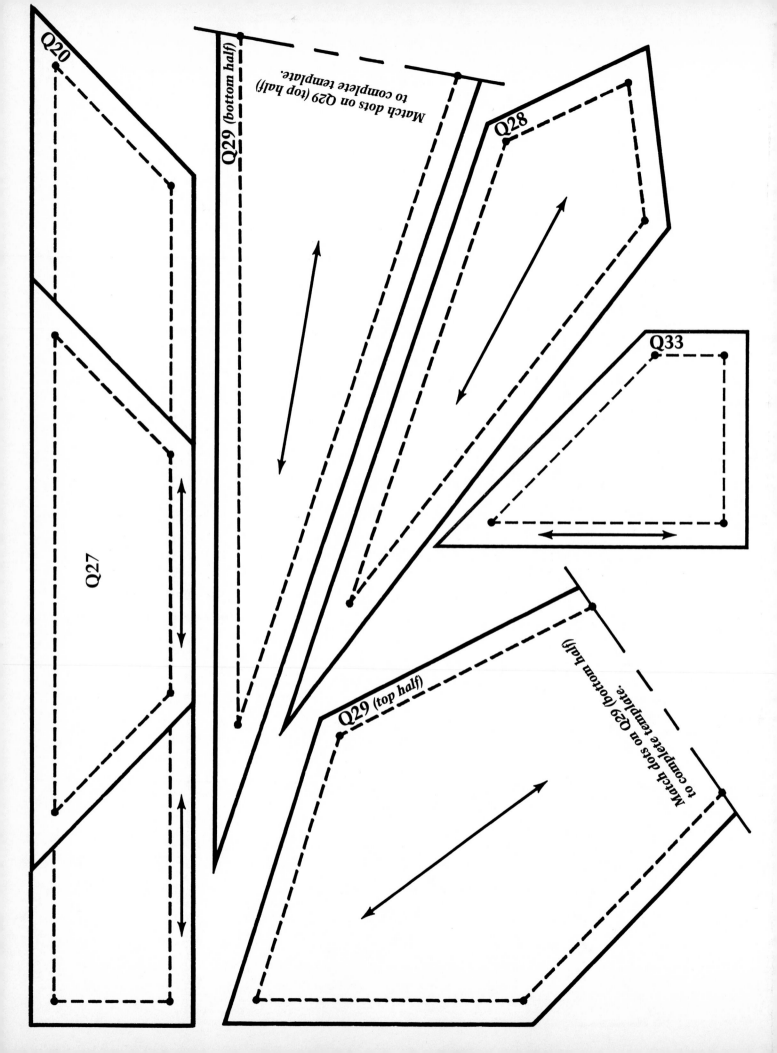

Q20

Q29 (bottom half)

Match dots on Q29 (top half)
to complete template.

Q28

Q33

Q27

Q29 (top half)

Match dots on Q29 (bottom half)
to complete template.

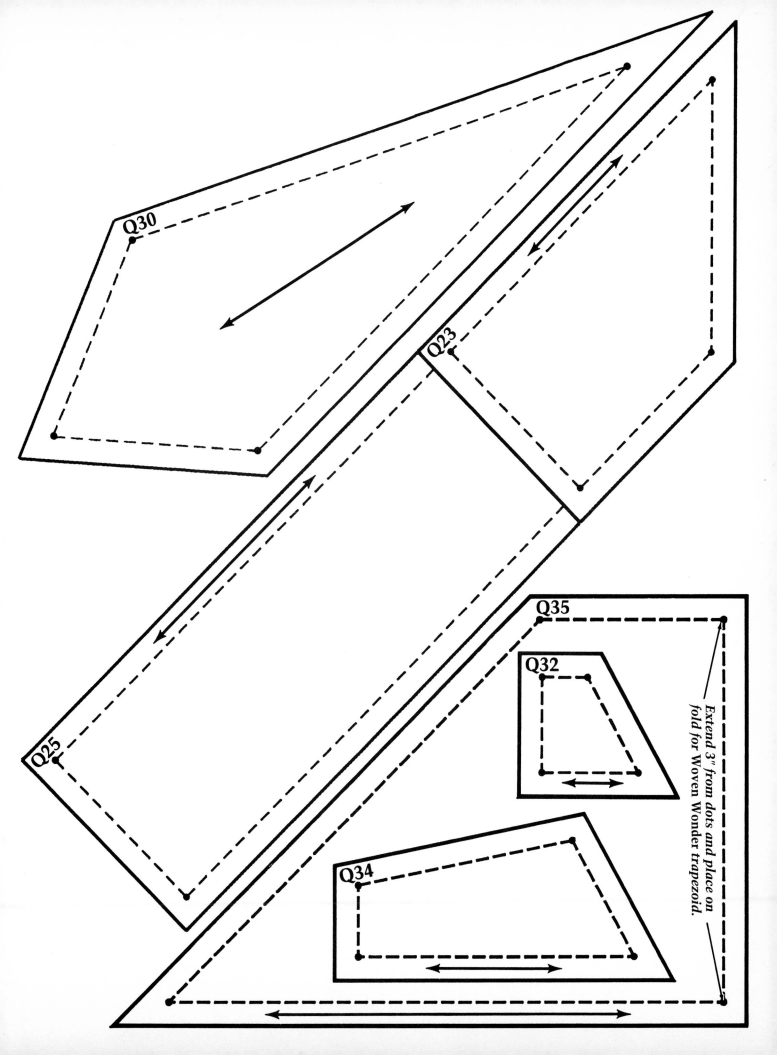

Q30

Q23

Q25

Q35

Q32

Q34

Extend 3" from dots and place on fold for Woven Wonder trapezoid.

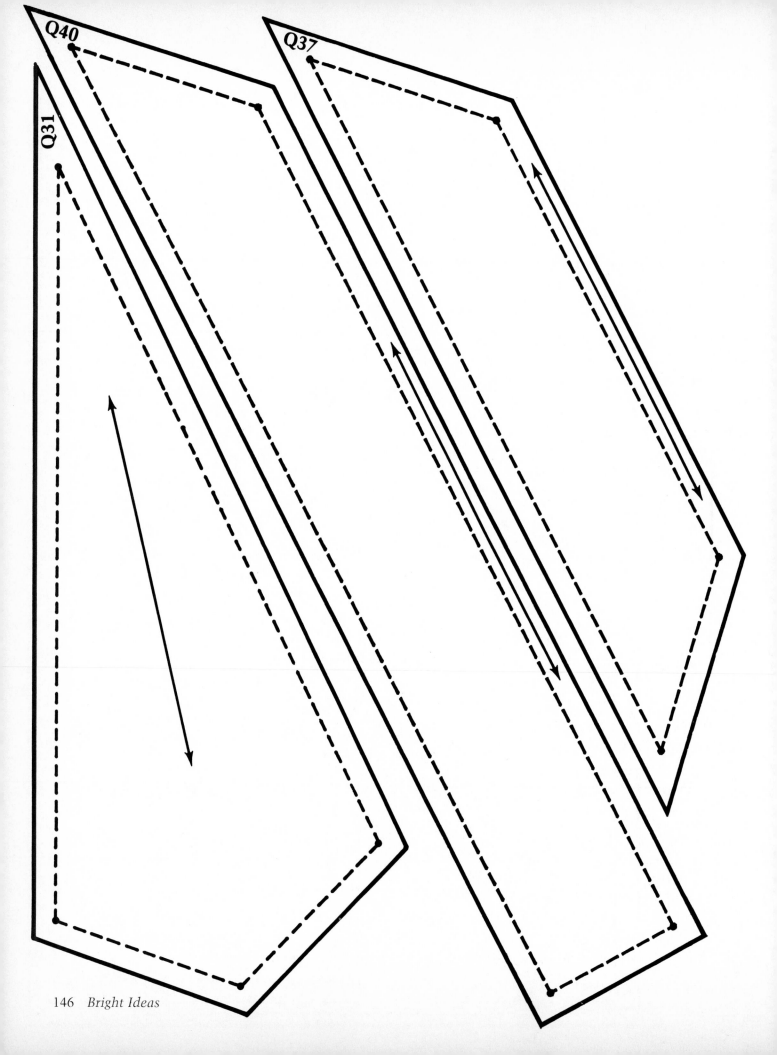

Q40

Q37

Q31

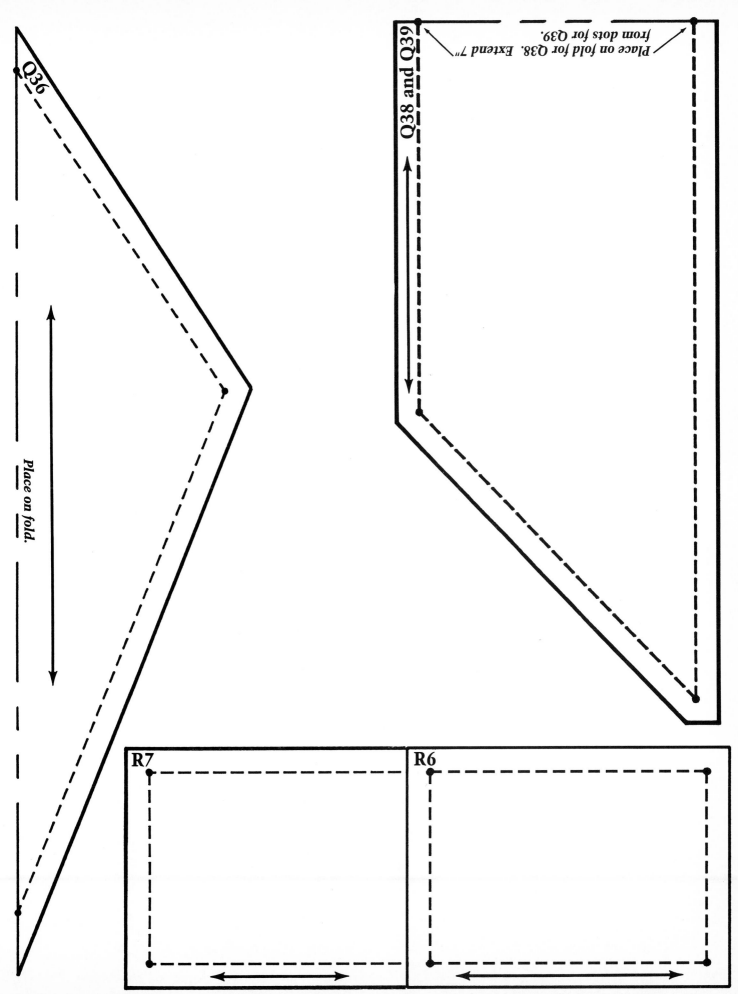

Q36

Place on fold.

Q38 and Q39

Place on fold for Q38. Extend 7" from dots for Q39.

R7

R6

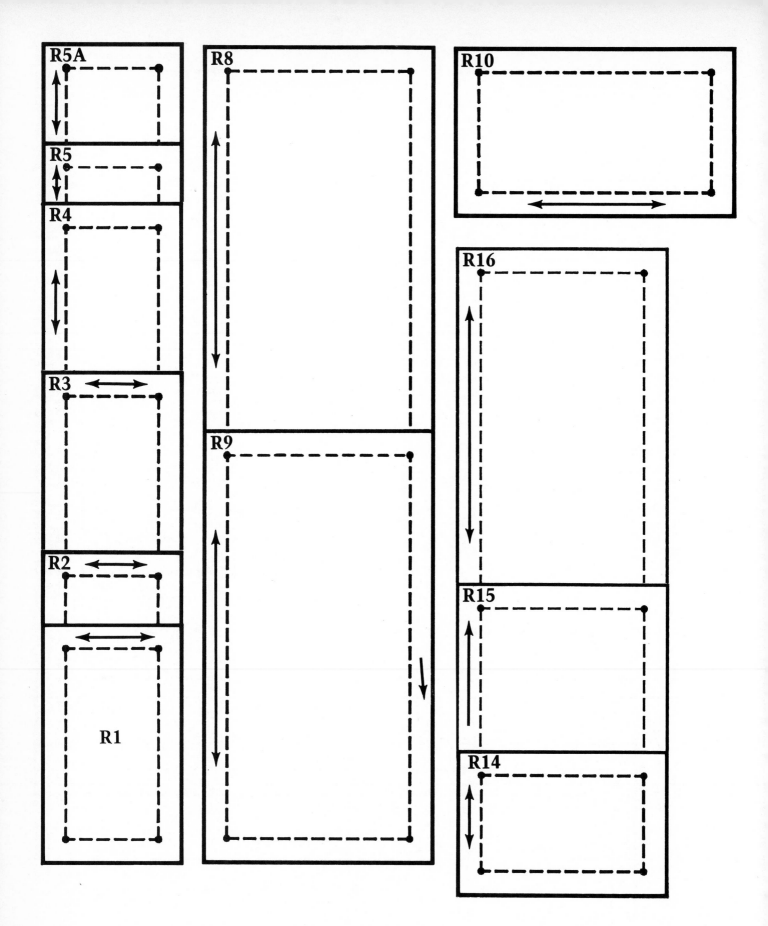

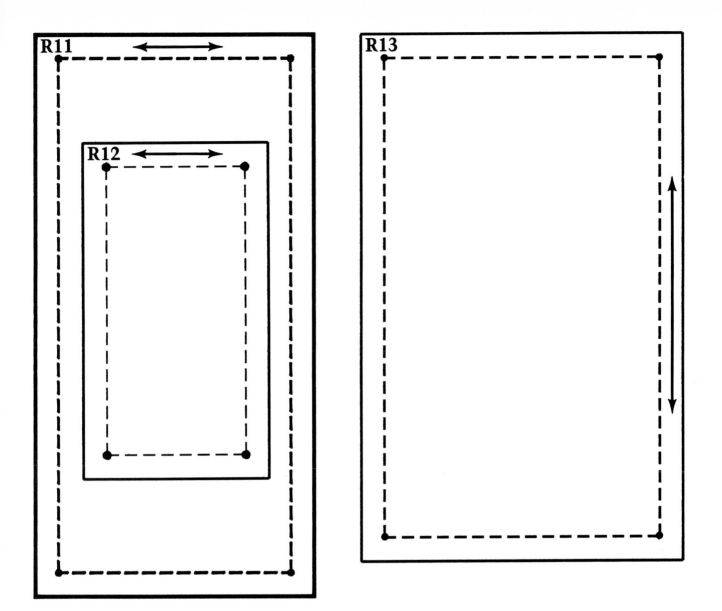

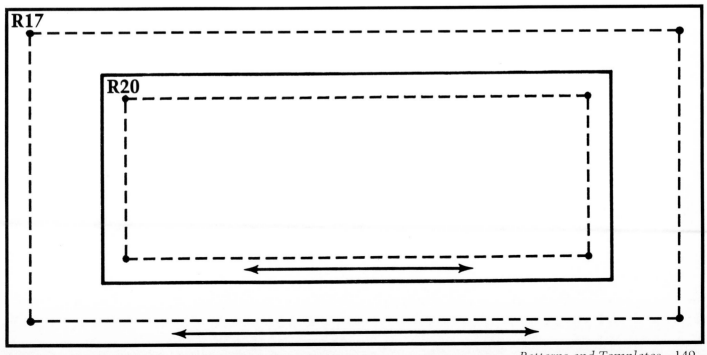

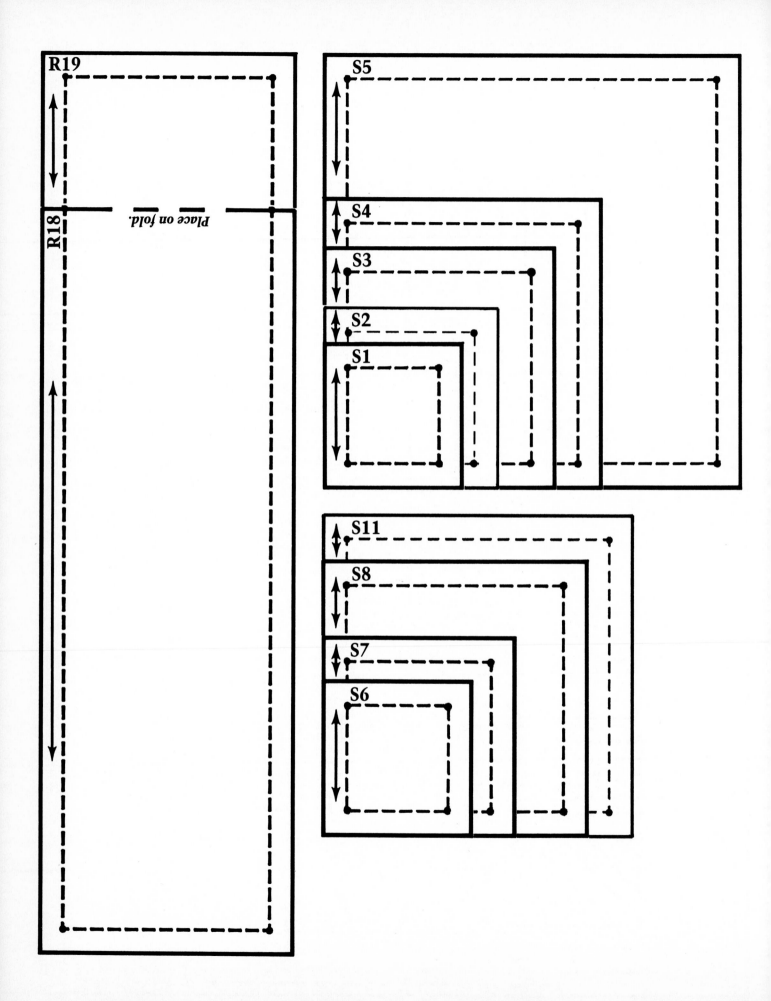

R19

R18

*Place on fold.*

S5

S4

S3

S2

S1

S11

S8

S7

S6

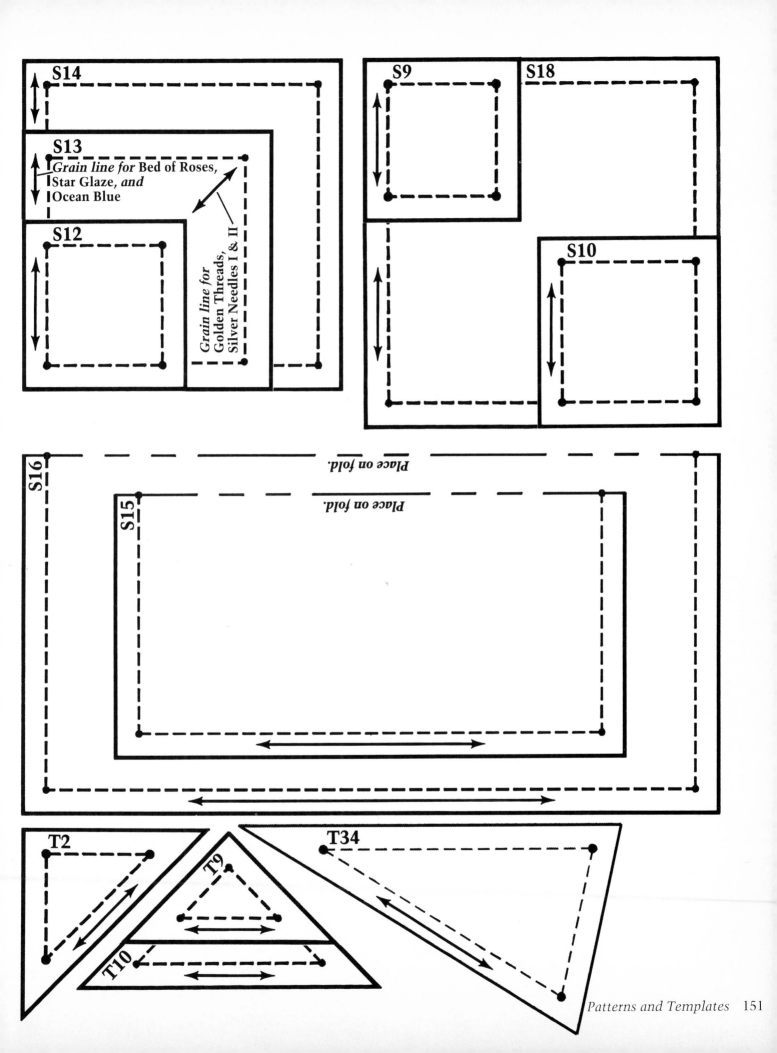

S14

S13

*Grain line for* Bed of Roses, Star Glaze, *and* Ocean Blue

*Grain line for* Golden Threads, Silver Needles I & II

S12

S9

S18

S10

S16

S15

*Place on fold.*

*Place on fold.*

T2

T9

T10

T34

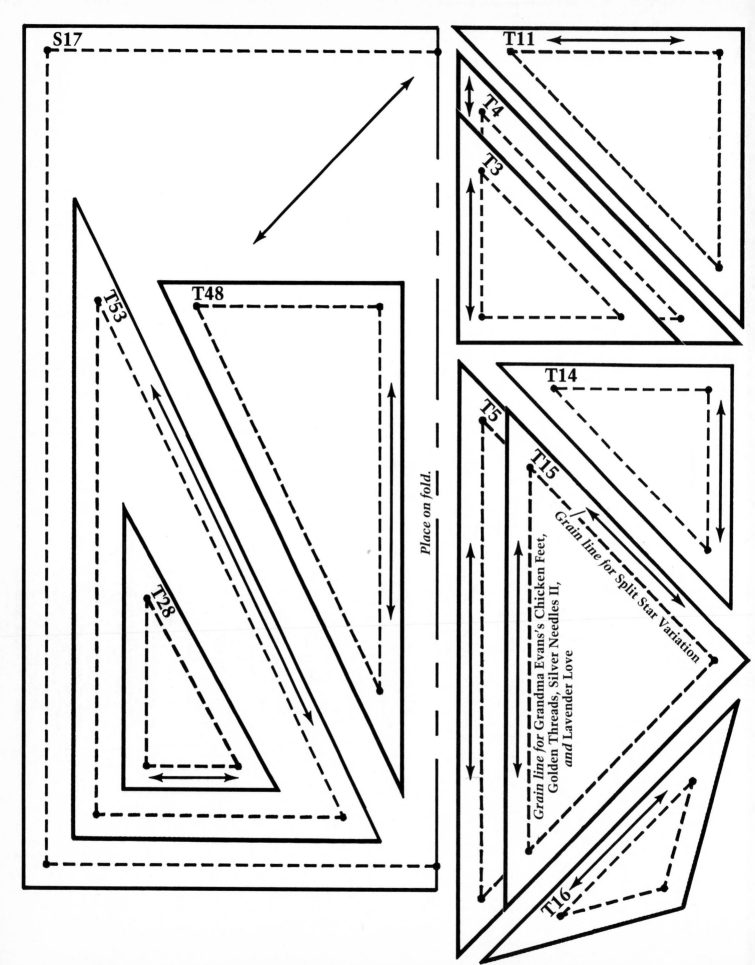

S17

T11

T4

T3

T53

T48

T28

Place on fold.

T14

T5

T15

Grain line for Grandma Evans's Chicken Feet,
Golden Threads, Silver Needles II,
and Lavender Love

Grain line for Split Star Variation

T16

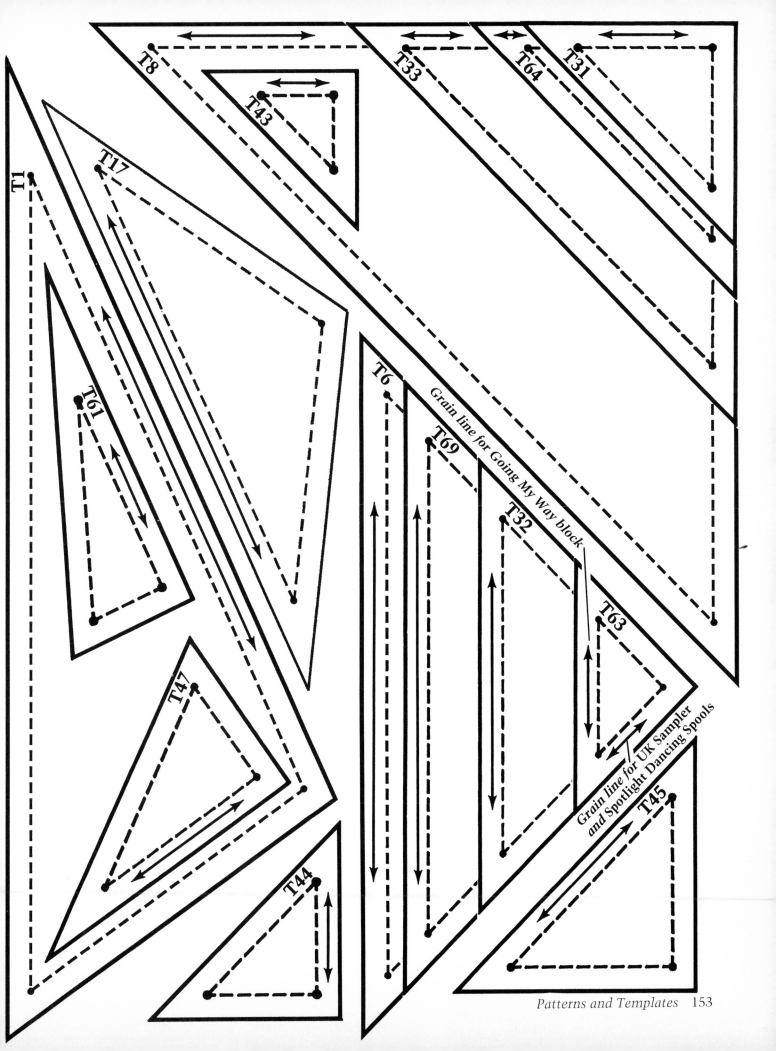

T8

T43

T33

T64

T31

T1

T17

T61

T6

T69

Grain line for Going My Way block

T32

T63

T47

Grain line for UK Sampler
and Spotlight Dancing Spools

T45

T44

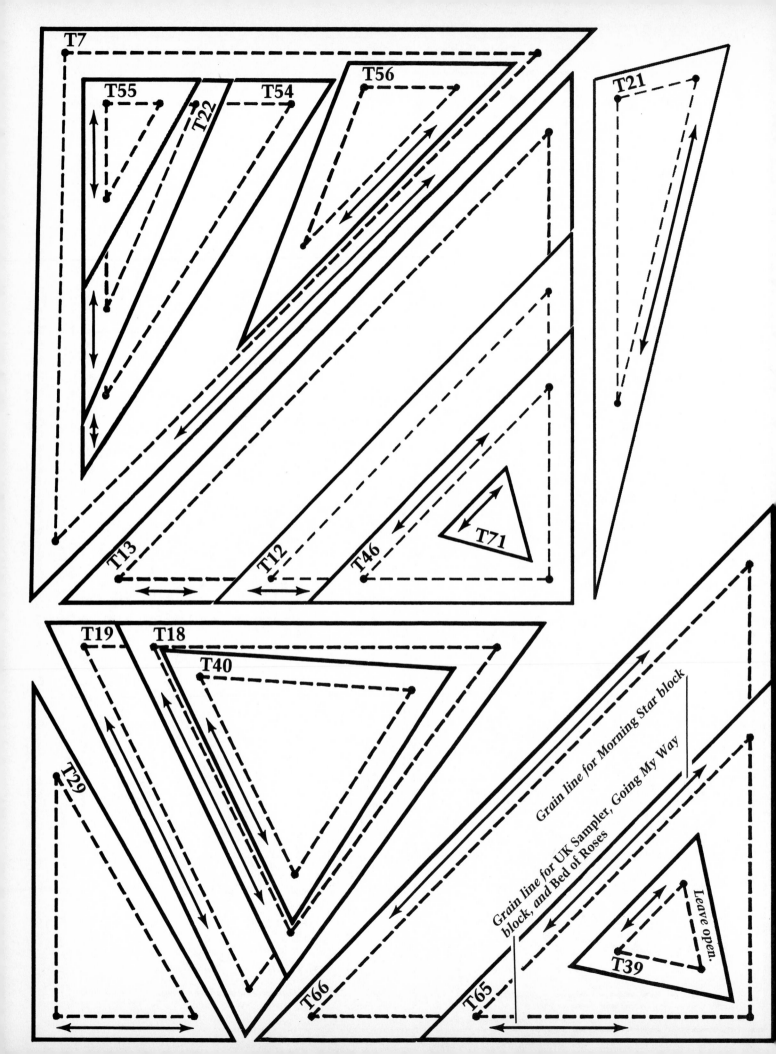

T7

T55

T22

T54

T56

T21

T13

T12

T46

T71

T19

T18

T40

T29

*Grain line for Morning Star block*

*Grain line for UK Sampler, Going My Way block, and Bed of Roses*

T66

T65

T39

*Leave open.*

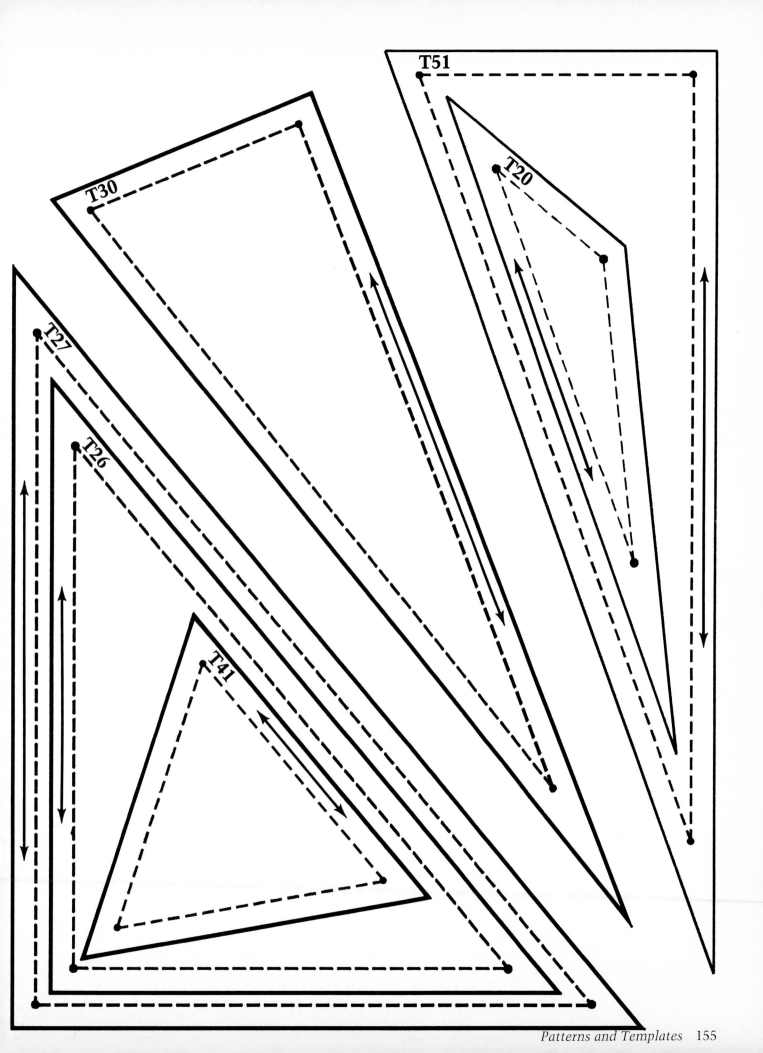

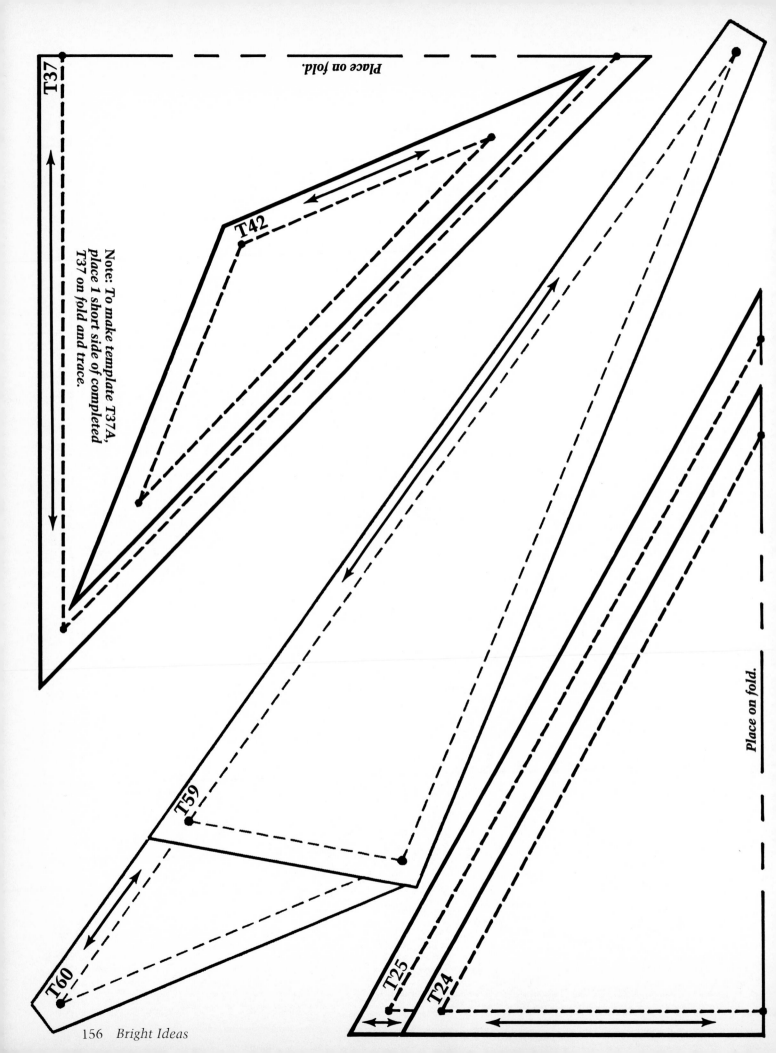

T37

Note: To make template T37A, place 1 short side of completed T37 on fold and trace.

*Place on fold.*

T42

T59

T60

T25

T24

*Place on fold.*

156   *Bright Ideas*

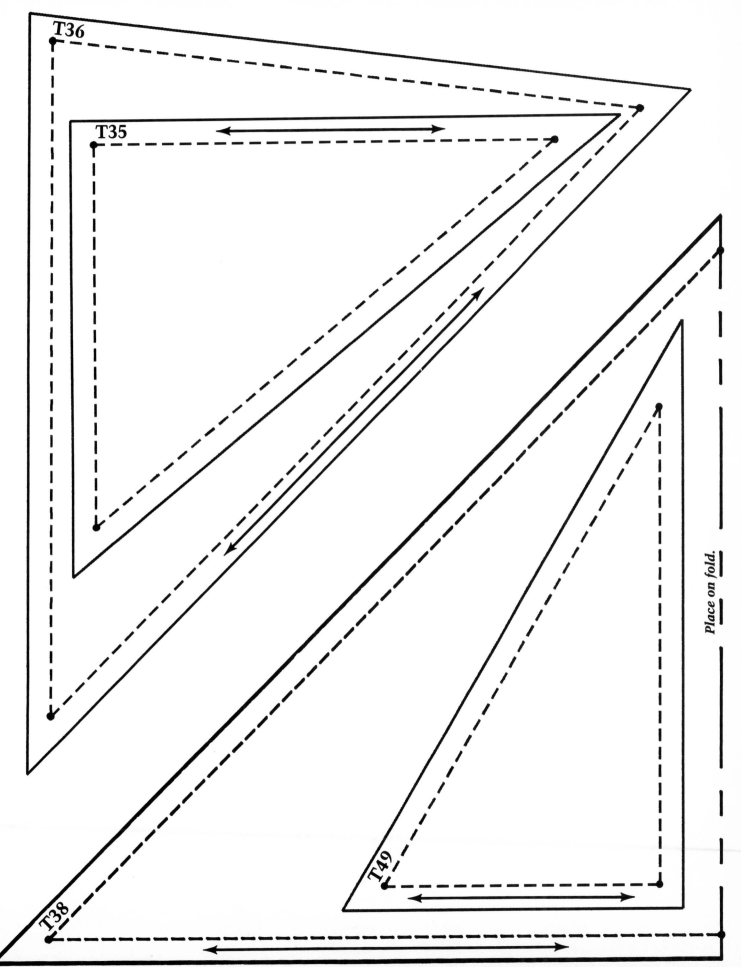

T36

T35

Place on fold.

T49

T38

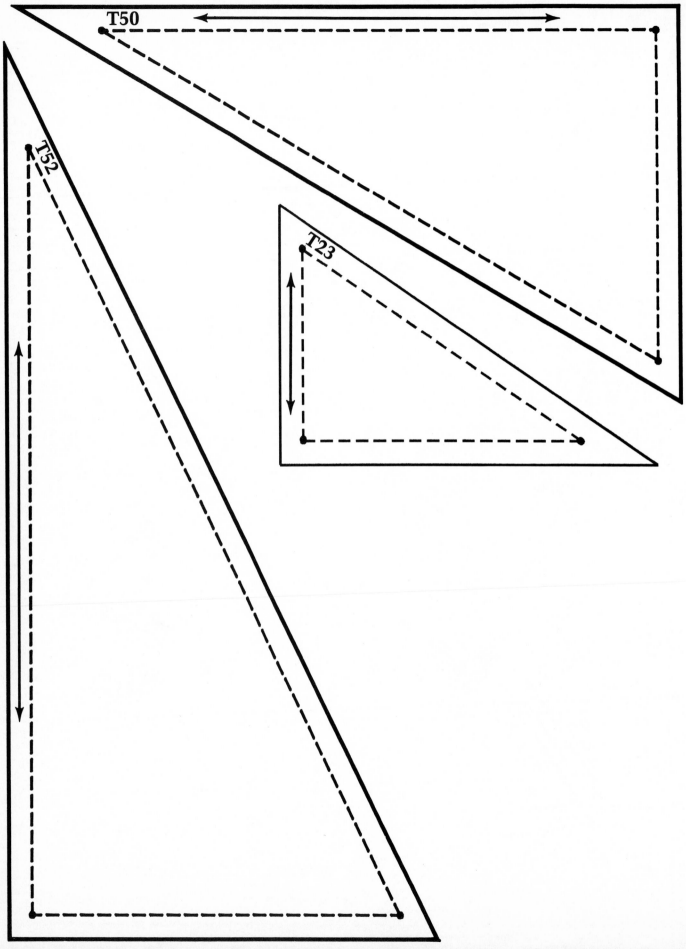

T50

T52

T23

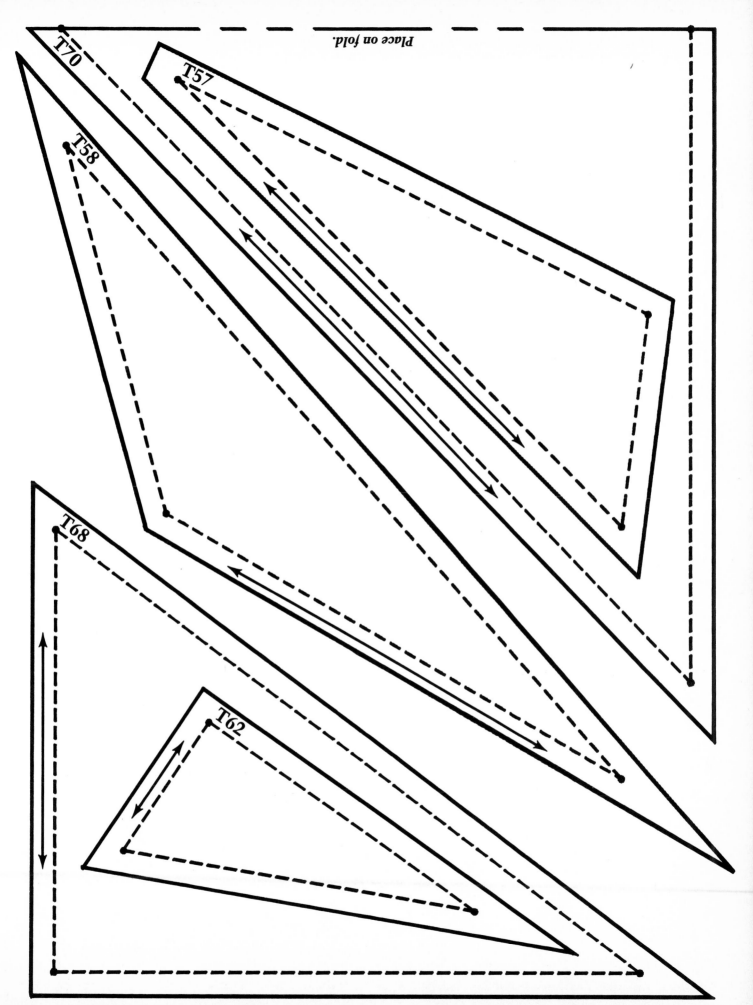

Place on fold.

T70

T57

T58

T68

T62

# CONTRIBUTORS

*Bricktown*, page 10; *Spotlight Dancing Spools*, page 19; *Plaid Pinwheels*, page 32; *Star Glaze*, page 34; *Copycat*, page 36; *Postage Stamp Pillow*, page 43; *Masks, Moose, and Qupak*, page 46; *Qupak Workshirt*, page 51; *Cruise and Quilt Banner*, page 52; *Moonbeams Over Many Ports*, page 56; *UK Sampler*, page 58; *Strawberries and Strings Vest*, page 77; *Interlock*, page 78; *Baby Buggy Boomers*, page 84; *Golden Threads, Silver Needles II*, page 92; *Car Star*, page 94; *Pastel Paisley Star*, page 96; *Split Star Variation*, page 98; *Lavender Love*, page 100; *Car Star Variation*, page 102; *Tea for Two Cozy*, page 108; *Quilting 'Round the Clock*, page 110; *Love Knot*, page 112; and *Modern Moon Over the Mountain*, page 118, designed, pieced, and quilted by Georgia Bonesteel.

*Dewey Decimal 746*, page 13, designed by Betsy Freeman; pieced and quilted by Landrum Library Quilters, Landrum, South Carolina.

*Bed of Roses*, page 16, designed, pieced, and quilted by Bloomington, Indiana, Quilters' Guild.

*Autumn Windows*, page 22, designed, pieced, and quilted by Alice Thomure.

*Little Toot*, page 24, designed, pieced, and quilted by Marilyn Fluharty.

*Hillside Village*, page 26, designed and pieced by Georgia Bonesteel; border pieced by Karol Roe; quilted by Linda Honsberger.

*Grandma Evans's Chicken Feet*, page 30, and *Singapore Stars*, page 62, designed, pieced, and quilted by Penny Wortman.

*Ocean Blue*, page 38, designed, pieced, and quilted by Maruszka V. Hufstader.

*The Ultimate Postage Stamp Quilt*, page 40, designed by Georgia Bonesteel; pieced and quilted by the Western North Carolina Quilters Guild.

*The Big Ship*, page 54, designed, pieced, and quilted by Georgia Bonesteel; sails by Karen Pervier, Helen Kelley, Doreen Speckman, and Virginia Avery.

*Amish Images*, page 66, designed and pieced by Georgia Bonesteel; quilted by Marie Detwiler and her quilting group from Princess Anne, Maryland.

*Hipp Strip*, page 72, designed, pieced, and quilted by Georgia Bonesteel; partial piecing by Joan Pierro and Peggy Genung.

*Woven Wonder*, page 74, designed by Georgia Bonesteel; pieced and quilted by Judy Rankin.

*Manteca Ribbons*, page 81, designed by Georgia Bonesteel; pieced and quilted by Manteca Quilters Guild, Manteca, California.

*Log Lanterns*, page 86, designed and pieced by Karen Pervier; quilted by Wendy Crigger.

*Golden Threads, Silver Needles I*, page 90, designed and pieced by Georgia Bonesteel; partial piecing by Glennda Gussman and Judy Rankin; special assistant, Virginia Jinkinson; quilted by Georgia Bonesteel and Linda Honsberger.

*House Exchange Program*, page 106, designed, pieced, and quilted by Georgia Bonesteel, Sheila Scawen, and the Freedom Escape Quilters.

*Decorator's Cover*, page 114, designed, pieced, and quilted by Jill Moore.

**Special thanks** to the following for sharing their homes, businesses, and resources: Susan Albers; Sara Jo and Jack Blackwood; Botanical Gardens of Birmingham; Mr. and Mrs. L. C. Boyd; Cabin Fever; Mr. and Mrs. Donald Chaney, Sr.; Children's Dance Foundation; Duke University Hospital; Mr. and Mrs. J. F. Egolf; Egolf Motors, Inc.; First Federal Savings Bank of Hendersonville; Donna Green; Mr. and Mrs. Ted Hipp; Ellen Hobbs; Honeysuckle Hollow Antiques; Mary-Gray Hunter; Lorna Katz; Ruth and Ed Lamonte; Mintz Brothers Builders; Mr. and Mrs. Ty Rhodes; Richard Tubb Interiors; Rich's; Alice Schleusner; Tom Shipman; Steve and Bunny Smith; Katie Stoddard; Barbara Stone; Ralph M. Terceira; Norma Thomas; Margery and Louis Wilhite; Mike Wilson; and Robert Wilson.

**For a free copy**
of *The Lap Quilter, Time-Tested Tools for Today's Quilter* from *Georgia Bonesteel*, send your name, address, and a first-class postage stamp to:
The Lap Quilter
P.O. Box 96,
Flat Rock, NC 28731.

**Other works by Georgia Bonesteel**
**Books**
   *Lap Quilting
      with Georgia Bonesteel*
   *More Lap Quilting
      with Georgia Bonesteel*
   *New Ideas for Lap Quilting*
**Video**
   *Lap Quilting
      with Georgia Bonesteel #1*
**Pattern Club**
   *Spinning Spools*

To find out how you can order *Cooking Light*® magazine, write to *Cooking Light*, P.O. Box C-549, Birmingham, AL 35283.